Henry Ward Beecher, Truman Jeremiah Ellinwood

A summer parish

Sabbath discourses and morning service of prayer

Henry Ward Beecher, Truman Jeremiah Ellinwood

A summer parish

Sabbath discourses and morning service of prayer

ISBN/EAN: 9783337257866

Printed in Europe, USA, Canada, Australia, Japan

Cover: Foto ©Lupo / pixelio.de

More available books at **www.hansebooks.com**

A SUMMER PARISH:

Sabbath Discourses,

AND

Morning Service of Prayer,

AT THE "TWIN MOUNTAIN HOUSE," WHITE MOUNTAINS, NEW HAMPSHIRE,
DURING THE SUMMER OF 1874,

By Henry Ward Beecher.

PHONOGRAPHICALLY REPORTED BY T. J. ELLINWOOD.

NEW YORK:
J. B. FORD AND COMPANY.
1875.

Entered according to Act of Congress, in the year 1874,
BY J. B. FORD AND COMPANY,
in the Office of the Librarian of Congress, at Washington.

PUBLISHER'S NOTICE.

For many years, Mr. Beecher has been accustomed to preach more or less in the neighborhoods which chanced to be his summer resting-places. During the past four summers he has taken refuge in the White Mountains from the annual hay-fever which relentlessly pursued him everywhere else; and, finding a congenial home at the "Twin Mountain House," he has been in the habit of preaching to the large family of guests in the parlors each Sunday morning.

For two summers, also, at the request of the guests, he has led the daily service of morning prayer, at the same time reading and familiarly commenting upon the Bible lesson.

Finding so wide and grateful an appreciation of Mr. Ellinwood's reports of Mr. Beecher's sermons, prayers, and lecture-room talks—a feeling which seems to grow broader and deeper with each succeeding year, and which very many letters from subscribers to the *Plymouth Pulpit* and the *Christian Union* have shown to be especially notable during the present year,—the publishers thought it well last season to secure reports of these informal discourses and family services, in what Mr. Beecher pleasantly calls his "summer parish." Hundreds of people, from every part of the land, and probably three of every other denomination to one of his own, were the friends who gathered every morning for the daily service of prayer, and every Sunday for the sermon.

This little book is put forth in the confident hope that it will be welcome to thousands of Mr. Beecher's friends everywhere, who will find interest in these, his lighter labors, during the period of gaining his summer rest.

J. B. Ford & Co.

New York, *May*, 1875.

CONTENTS.

Sermons.

		PAGE
I.	WHAT IS RELIGION?	7
	LESSON: Gal. v. 1-13. *HYMNS: Nos. 888, 705, Doxology.	
II.	CHRISTIAN SYMPATHY	29
	LESSON: Rom. xii. HYMNS: Nos. 102, 632.	
III.	LUMINOUS HOURS	55
	LESSON: Luke ix. 28-42. HYMNS: Nos. 119, 564, Doxology.	
IV.	LAW AND LIBERTY	81
	LESSON: Luke ix., 28-42. HYMNS: Nos. 31, 1166, Doxology.	
V.	"AS A LITTLE CHILD."	103
	HYMNS: Nos. 776, 733, Doxology.	

Services of Morning Prayer.

I.	PAUL'S IDEA OF LOVE	137
	LESSON: 1 Cor. xiii. HYMN: No. 770.	
II.	THE VALUE OF MANKIND	147
	LESSON: Mark ii. HYMN: No. 823.	
III.	THE CHASTISEMENTS OF LOVE	155
	LESSON: Heb. xii. 1-13. HYMN: No. 733.	
IV.	NEIGHBORLINESS	167
	LESSON: Luke x. 25-37. HYMN: No. 424.	

* PLYMOUTH COLLECTION.

V. HEAVEN . . . .
   LESSON: Heb. xii. 18-20. *HYMN: No. 545.

VI. PICTURES OF TRUTH . . . . .
   LESSON: Rev. v. HYMN: No. 346.

VII. SCRIPTURE LESSON; without comment .
   LESSON: Phil. ii. 1-16. HYMN: No. 704.

VIII. CHRISTIAN LIVING . . . . . .
   LESSON: Rom. xii. HYMN: "Shining Shore".

IX. ONE WITH CHRIST . . . . . .
   LESSON: John xv. 5-13. HYMNS: Nos. 837, 424.

X. SPIRITUAL CONCEIT . . . .
   LESSON: Luke xv. 1-32. HYMN: No. 840.

XI. CHRIST, THE PHYSICIAN . . . .
   LESSON: Luke xix. HYMN: No. 808.

XII. MAN-LOVING, THE ROAD TO GOD-LOVING .
   LESSON: John xiii. 1-17. HYMN: No. 776.

* PLYMOUTH COLLECTION.

Sermons.

I.

WHAT IS RELIGION?

WHAT IS RELIGION?

I shall take for a starting point, in the remarks that I make this morning, the 19th verse of the 2d chapter of the 2d Epistle to Timothy:

"Nevertheless the foundation of God standeth sure, having this seal, The Lord knoweth them that are his."

The context is this:

"Who concerning the truth have erred, saying that the resurrection is past already; and overthrow the faith of some. Nevertheless the foundation of God standeth sure."

We have come in our day into times precisely like those of the apostle, in which there is a great movement throughout the whole civilized world, and a great change of feeling, an apprehension or what is worse, in regard to the stability of the Christian religion.

There are two classes that look upon this matter from very different standpoints. On the one side are those who are devout philosophers in religion, and who hear doctrines which seem to them to be very strange expositions of Christianity—doctrines which they have not been accustomed to. They see the manners and customs of religious institutions or churches very much disturbed; and they have an impression that evil is coming in like a flood, that the foundations are being removed, that the old landmarks are being taken out of the way, that everything is going to wreck and ruin, and that rank infidelity, atheism and anarchy are going to overflow the world.

Then, on the other extreme, there are those who feel that religion is not worth anything at all if it stands on foundations of the past; but that it is like an old stubble-field, that

---

Preached at the TWIN MOUNTAIN HOUSE, White Mountains, N. H., Sunday morning, August 23d, 1874. Lesson: Gal. v., 1-13. Hymns (Plymouth Collection): Nos. 888, 705, Doxology.

it was valuable one or two thousand years ago, that some wheat was reaped from it then, but that what was good in it has been gathered out, and that we are coming, by progress, to a new era. Some think it is to be an era of spiritualism, in which there are to be glimpses of light and knowledge from other spheres; and yet, what foundation it is to stand upon they do not know, though they think it will stand on something.

In sympathy with these, or in antagonism to them, as the case may be, there is a host of men who believe that science is breaking the seal, and that the things of God, hidden from the foundations of the world, are now being made known through the ministrations of science; and they say, "Away with your superstitions and dogmas and doctrines! They may once have been helpful; but the time has come for the shining of truth through science."

So, in these different ways — some out of fear for the integrity of religious things, and some with the hope that there is to be a far more blessed day of knowledge than ever before, and almost all, I think, with an amiable, kind, humane feeling—this great outlying, skirting host are of opinion that religion is pretty much done up, and that we are now to look for something better.

To all such I say, The foundations of God stand yet, firm and sure; and I declare that the essential elements of Christianity were never so apparent as to-day; that they were never so influential; that they were never so likely to produce institutions of power; that they never had such a hold on human reason and human conscience; and that the religious impulse of the human race was never so deep, and never so strong in its current.

In the first place, then, we must recollect that there may be very great changes around about religion, in its external forms, without any essential interior change, nay, even with the augmentation of its interior power. I will admit that there has been a great change of the forms in which facts have been woven into doctrines. In other words, the great outlying facts of human consciousness—the nature of man; the character of intelligence and of volition; the truths of responsibility and moral government; what they are; how they are to be brought together into a perfect system; the existence of God and of a divine providence—all these things have been held in various ways, and have been philosophically stated in different forms; and that there has been, and is yet to be, a great change in the mode of stating these things, I do not deny; but I hold that their statement is one which grows better and better from age to age. Some men think that anything which is a revelation from God must be always one and the same thing; but God's revelation is alphabetic; it is a revelation of letters, and they can be combined and recombined in ten thousand different words, varying endlessly. The great facts which are fundamental to consciousness, once being given, are alphabetic; and these facts may be combined; and with the development of the human race in intelligence and moral excellence they go on taking new forms; and larger experiences must have a larger expression. The trouble with a statement in an early age is, that while it is true to the sum of the knowledge of that age, each age develops an individuality of its own, knowledge making it larger; and a statement must be made which is as large as the actual experience of the human soul has been.

Take agriculture. In the earliest period of the settlement of a neighborhood, men clear a piece containing a few acres of ground, and put such a fence around it as they can afford, and plow among the stumps, and leave them standing; but as time goes on the stumps disappear, and in twenty or thirty years, when they are gone, a man, coming back, and missing them, says, "Why, where are those precious stumps that I remember used to be in this field? The boys have easy times plowing now-a-days; but when I was a boy it meant something to plow among those stumps and their roots. This is not what I call farming. You are all going to effeminacy." It is not such farming as he was used to; but it is better than the farming that belonged to primitive times, which may have had its pleasant memories and associations, but which was not farming in its highest form. Has not agriculture grown? Has it lost ground because the fences and the plows are better than they were at the beginning, and because one man can now do as much as ten men then could? Has agriculture gone under because its instruments are changed, and because its forms are different? Is not the change it has undergone a sign of advancement and improvement?

So, in the knowledges of the world, and in its various institutions, there have been changes, and there are to be changes; but they are progressive. On the whole, they are not ominous of evil, but are full of fructifications of hope.

The changes of religious institutions trouble people; and if I supposed that the church was an exactly ordered institution, I should be troubled about its changes; but according to my understanding it is not such an institution.

When an architect has drawn the plan of a house, or a public building, his lines are laid down just so, his measurements are precise, and he specifies whether it shall be of wood or brick or stone; and the contract is made according to the specifications, and the builder has to follow them.

Now, there are many who think that the church was sent to us in that way, that there are just such lines and measurements laid down respecting it, and that we are bound to follow those lines and measurements. They think that exact ordinances are prescribed, and that we are under obligation to observe them.

If I believed this, I should look upon the innovations of modern times as dangerous; but I do not believe the church was ordained to be in a particular shape any more than I believe that schools were. I do not believe that the New Testament prescribes that our ordinances and methods of worship shall take on any given form. I do not believe that the rules and regulations of the church were made precise and specific any more than those of town meetings, or the constitutions of the several States, or the Constitution of the United States were. Government is ordained in the nature of man, and it begins to operate, and men find out among themselves, by their experience, that their government is to be formed and administered largely according to the climate and physical characteristics of the country where they are, the degree of civilization which they have attained, and the exigencies of national life as they arise.

The same is true of religious institutions. I believe that God ordained the church. That is to say, when he made men he made them social beings, so that no man can live without wanting to touch his fellow men somewhere. It is the necessities of men's social natures that have led them to come together in churches.

When patriotism swells in the hearts of men, and sets them on fire, no man wants to be alone in the field, and he seeks his neighbor, who joins him; and the villagers unite together; and the more intense men's feelings are, the more they run to each other. For we are not born to be separate drops, but drops united together to form streams, with channels deep and wide, and with impetuous currents. When God made men with social natures, he ordained that they should come together by their loves, by their tastes, by their enthusiasms; and that ordination is the foundation on which the church stands. It is decreed that you shall come together with your aspiration, with your devotion, with your affection, with your hope.

So God created the church; but whether it should be Presbyterian, or Methodist, or Baptist, or Congregational, or Episcopalian, or Roman Catholic—God has never troubled himself about that, though his zealous disciples have. The form of the instrument of religion is not a part of his decrees. He no more ordained that divine worship should be carried on in certain fixed ways than he ordained that men who live by agriculture should harrow or furrow their fields. Agriculture does not stand on the machines which it employs, but on the necessity of men to eat. When God made men hungry he foreordained agriculture. And in the matter of the church, it does not stand on its ordinances.

But do not think that I am speaking contemptuously of these things. What I desire to be understood as saying is, that men have no business to worship an ordinance. I say that men have no right to make an idol of the church, or of Sunday, or of the Bible, or of anything that is in itself an instrument. Religion is something other than the instrument by which it is produced.

Do I say my prayers to the school-house? No. And yet,

I believe in intelligence; and the school is simply an instrument by which we develop that intelligence. Do I say my prayers to the arithmetic, the geography, and the grammar? No. I think they are useful; but I would kick them every one out of the house if you were to tell me that I must say my prayers to them. They are my servants, my helps, but not my masters.

And so, when men open the doors of the sanctuary on Sunday, the church is not my master: I am its master, for I am a son of God. It is simply the chariot which he has sent to carry me on my journey.

When a minister stands to teach me, is he my master? No. If he can help me, well and good. Like other men, he is to be estimated according to what he can do. What he is, that am I. I am a sinner before God, living on God's mercy and goodness, and that is he. No ordination, no long line of influences, though ten thousand times ten thousand years should rest on his head, would make a man anything but a man. And when he ceases to be a man, he dies, and is gone. All men that live have the same passions and appetites; human nature is the same everywhere; and ministers have their pride, their vanity, their weaknesses and their temptablenesses; they are all just common men; and God never put one of them over his fellows, or made him superior to them. Still less did God ever say to an ordinance, "Go down and stand in the midst of men, and make them bow to you." Therefore, not to the refluent waves, nor to the sprinkling drops, nor to any instrument, will I bow down, and say, "Ye are my master." God is my master; and to these things I say, "Ye are my servants;" and I look down on them all.

Now, when I see that there is change in the institutions of religion, in the currents of government, and in the ordinances of the church, I do not stand quivering, and saying, "Men have departed from the counsels of God, and religion is going to destruction, and we do not know where it will end." I say that religion lies, not in outside things, but in the states of men's minds. It is the way that they think and feel and act that determines what their religion is. Religion is human experience. It is the soul's action God-ward and man-ward. And if religion is going out of the world, it is not because the old church is unshingled, nor because the familiar bell has stopped swinging in the belfry, nor because men are indifferent to forms, nor because they do not care for the Book, nor because the ministry is not revered as it used to be. These things may be fortunate or unfortunate, according to circumstances; but religion will not have died out of the world until it has died out of the human soul. Religion is the experience of human souls in their relations to God. Sympathy toward God and men—that is religion; and whether that is decreasing or increasing in power throughout the world will not be judged by these external signs or measurements, but by other and very different ones.

It is said that men do not believe in virtue. Well, when a man tells me that the refinements of the school-men are lapsing on questions which relate to eternal regeneration through the Son of God, and that many of the fine distinctions between ability-natural and ability-spiritual are going out of men's thoughts and out of much use, I admit it; but I say that the great fundamental truths of religion—namely, the nature of man, the wants of man, and divine love as a sufficient supply for human wants—instead of growing weaker are growing stronger in men's minds.

There has been a great deal of teaching in regard to the depravity of man. I think I could preach to you a doctrine of total depravity, after the old fashioned sort, which would make every one of you red in the face, and angry, so that you would say, "I do not believe a word of it;" and I think I could preach to you what men tried to preach in the olden time on that subject so that you would not one of you deny it.

For example, every man is born at zero. He is nothing at first. We are told that men are born without original righteousness; but this is not half of it; they are born without original anything, except a little sack of pulpy matter. The supreme function at birth is suction. Men are born without a name and without a trade. They are born without power to walk, without power to handle anything, without power to see, and without power to hear. Their senses are not born until they have been in the world months and months. It is a mere seed that is born. When, therefore, I am told that men are born without original righteousness, I do not find any difficulty in believing that; for they are born without anything. They do not feel nor think. They are a bundle of capacities susceptible of development by-and-by. There is not one element in that wonderful, obscure, undeveloped thing called a *baby*, which is not unfolded by the law of gradualism, little by little, step by step. We do not learn to see except by experience in seeing. The eye is all right; but it is to be trained for its function. We cannot stretch out the hand, or bring it back, or do anything with it until we have learned to use it.

There is a jubilee in the family when the child first walks. The father comes home at night, and the mother says, "Oh, baby has walked! baby has walked!" Yes, it has walked; but it had to practice a great while before it could get up, and stand on its feet, and take one step after another without falling. Walking has to be learned; and when the child has learned to walk, what infinite slappings there are to teach it to not walk where it ought not to! How we strive to teach the child to talk! and then how we rebuke him because he talks too much, or at the wrong times! How much time is spent in teaching him how to reach out his hand! and then how his hand gets whipped when he reaches it out and puts it into the sweet-meats! Everything is taught, and everything comes by practice, in these matters.

When, therefore, it is said that men are born in a deplorable state of wickedness, and that there is no original righteousness, you accept it as much as the old divines used to. You state it differently, but you recognize it. It is inherent in human nature. Nobody can deny it as it is stated and explained now, and nobody is disposed to.

But that is not all; it is not possible for man, beginning at nothing, to unfold and grow up to something, without making many mistakes. The child does not walk perfectly at the outset; it is not possible that he should; and you do not set it down against him. The child is not able to use his hand at once; but nobody sets that down against him. It is a part of God's original design in the world that men shall be born at the seminal point, and grow up gradually toward perfection; and that being the original design, imperfection is a part of it.

As no man can use his eye except he has been drilled to do it, and as no man can use his hand except he has been drilled to do that, so no man can use his reason without having been taught to use it. When the child goes to school, and undertakes to learn to write, the master, if he fails to make a round and beautiful O, does not say to him, "That is total depravity. You ought to write right." We wait for a child that is learning to write, and give him a chance to become proficient by practice. Early imperfections are not necessarily blameworthy. They are largely inherent, and necessary to the conditions in which men are placed in this world by the creative fiat of God himself. When a child begins to learn a trade we expect him to spoil tools. When a young man commences to do carpenter's work we do not find fault with him because he does not shove the plane just so, or use the saw in the best manner, or make his joints exactly right. We wait for him to learn these things. The process of learning a trade is called *apprenticeship*. We have an apprenticeship for the hand, an apprenticeship for the foot, an apprenticeship for the eye, and an apprenticeship for the ear. When a man learns arithmetic and grammar he goes through an apprenticeship of the reason. And do not you think that there is an apprenticeship for the affections and the moral sentiments? There is; and it is harder to develop the higher powers in the soul than it is to develop the lower; it takes longer; and it is attended with more imperfections; and these imperfections are a part of God's foreseeing wisdom.

Just here comes in the distinction between infirmities or faults, and transgressions or sins. The Scriptures recognize a difference in them. Wrong things done on purpose are sins; and those things which fall out from inexperience, from not knowing, from weakness or from imperfection, are faults. Imperfections inhere in the whole divine conception of the human race on the globe; and men are filled with infirmities, of necessity; and these infirmities break out into transgressions more or less complicated all the way down.

Now, I have been stating facts; but suppose that I should say to you, "The doctrine of the Bible is that men are sinful; and so sinful that they all need to be born again"? I do teach that doctrine, in its totality. Everybody is imperfect. Everybody sins with every part of his mind. Nobody ever becomes manly and strong except by an overruling influence that inspires him, and lifts him up from the lower plane to the higher.

And so, after all the pother that is made about the doctrines of human depravity, and the need of regeneration by the power of the Holy Ghost, are they not true? Men kick them about like so many foot-balls; but do they not recognize them as true when they are stated in a different way from that in which they have been accustomed to hear them stated, and in a way which is suited to the experience of our times? To us the old doctrines may seem to be dying, but the old human nature is just the same everywhere. Men are empty, and do not know how to do right things till they have learned; and they learn painfully, and under circumstances in which they want divine inspiration; for no man rises from a low plane to the higher one of heroism and enthusiasm without the aid of a higher mind than his own.

Men think these truths are passing out of the world; but I say they are simply taking another form of exposition. The truths themselves are inherent, universal, indestructible.

I think that if there be any one thing that has been misinterpreted, it is the doctrine of the divine influence upon the human soul. As I recollect my own belief when I was a child—and I was an orthodox child—I believed that when a man who was born a sinner, and who had grown up in sin, came to a certain age, and went through a proper fermentation, and had dejected the lees, as it were, and left the wine of life pretty clear above, he was converted. I believed that he then passed from the north side of the hedge, where it was shady, to the south side, where the sun always shone. I believed that God shone on his elect, that they had the divine influence, and that no others had. But my impression now is, that there is not a single human soul that is not the product of the divine Spirit, and that that Spirit is the vivific element of the universe; and that as the sun in spring knocks at the tomb of every sleeping plant, and there is a resurrection wherever there is a bud or germ, and there is not a daisy or harebell, or ranunculus, or flower of any kind that does not start at the solicitation of the sun's light and warmth, so the roots of power being here in human souls, there must be a shining of the divine Soul directly upon them to bring out in them intelligence, emotions, and moral sentiments. This down-shining influence of God is universal.

What, does the Spirit of God help men before conversion? Oh, yes; all men, always and everywhere—the savage and the semi-civilized as well as the civilized. All men, whatever may be their nature, are under the divine guidance of providence, and of the stimulating influence of the divine Spirit. All may not profit by it as much as we do, but it is as much for them as for us. All do not profit by the sun alike, but the sun shines as much for one as for another. Some are lazy and some are industrious; and it depends upon each one how far he shall derive benefit from the life-giving power of the sun. How much profit shall be enjoyed by each one is determined, not by the sun, but by the man who receives its light and heat. The sun means gold to one man, and mud to another. It means active energy to one man, and sitting in the corner of laziness to another. The sun is not to blame if men do not take its bounty.

And so inspiration comes to all men. Those who receive what they can take in of it are thus prepared to receive more, and to be made better and better by it. And I think that this doctrine of divine inspiration and down-shining, instead of being less believed than ever before, is more believed. It is taking on some extravagant forms and modes of expression; its philosophy is not always the wisest and best; but I think there is a prevalent growing feeling that God is nearer to the human race now than he was in the past; that he is the universal Father of mankind; that those limitations and distinctions which exist among men are a part of

God's original design; and that more men are coming to him, and coming in more ways, than ever before.

Do not think that you are the only men that pray. Drunkards pray. There is not a man here who has put up such anguishful petitions to God as some men have who are very bad in the sight of the world. Do you suppose that men who are bad go down without prickings of conscience, and without many yearnings for the interposition of God's power? I tell you, the struggles of men who are going down to death are often a thousand times more admirable in the sight of God than the easy efforts of men naturally born to virtue. It was the one that was lost that God thought of more than of the ninety and nine just persons who needed no repentance; and I think the prevalent feeling is that God never was nearer to men, and never more helpful toward them, and never dearer to them than to-day. The first truth is the Fatherhood of God; the next is the brotherhood of man; and I think they were never before so prevalent and vital as they are to-day.

But look at it in another way. Take the elements of religion; it is not one thing alone. It means the moving of the human soul rightly toward God, toward man, and toward duty. He who is using his whole self according to laws of God is religious. Some men think that devotion is religion. Yes, devotion is religion; but it is not all of religion. Here is a tune written in six parts; and men are wrangling and quarreling about it. One says that the harmony is in the bass, another that it is in the soprano, another that it is in the tenor, and another that it is in the alto; but I say that it is in all the six parts. Each may, in and of itself, be better than nothing; but it requires the whole six parts to make what was meant by the musical composer. Some men say that love is religion. Well, love is, certainly, the highest element of it; but it is not that alone. Justice is religion; fidelity is religion; hope is religion; faith is religion; obedience is religion. These are all part and parcel of religion. Religion is as much as the total of manhood; and it takes in every element of it. All the elements of manhood, in their right place and action, are constituent parts of religion; but no one of them alone is religion. It takes the whole manhood, imbued and inspired of God, moving right both heavenward and earthward, to constitute religion.

Many men think that a man who shudders and trembles with a sense of the presence of the Most High, who is so devout that he lays his hand on his mouth and his mouth in the dust, and cries, "Unclean, unclean; God be merciful to me a sinner," is a very religious man; but that depends upon circumstances. I have known men who went into a mood in which they were profoundly struck through with veneration when under religious influences, but who could not resist temptation in business, and would cheat, and would get the best of a bargain, and justify themselves by their love of others. They said, "I love my neighbor as myself,"— that was for Sunday; and they also said, "Every man for himself,"—that was for Monday, and the other week days.

But you find men who, in conference meetings and church meetings, or when the bell sounds, or when the organ peals, have reverent feelings, and in whom, under such circumstances, worldly feelings do subside. They go to church, and when they come to the church door they take off their hat, and march to their seat, looking neither to the right nor to the left, and bow themselves down, and go through the whole religious service, and rise, and go out, and feel that they have been religious; and they see boys pouring out of the church on the other side of the street, talking and laughing, and they shudder to think what an irreligious and godless generation of children is growing up. They have been doing their religion; and it is ink-color; it is dark and somber. But do I revile it? Do I say it is incongruous and inconsistent with Christian hope? In its place it is as much right as either part in a piece of music is right. The sub-bass is all right in an organ; but I should not want a man to play on a thirty-two foot pipe all the time and tell me that that was music.

There are other men who think that religion is a proper view of the whole scheme of Gospel truth. They·lift their spectacles up from their sharp, gray eyes, and begin at the beginning, and lay down position after position, and squint along the line; and if it lacks a thousandth part of an inch, they think there is heresy. Orthodoxy to them is right belief at every post and corner. This is intellectual religion. But do I ridicule it? No, not in its place and position. There is no man that is a man who does not think; and if he thinks he must connect his thoughts together; and if he thinks about religion, his thoughts must form a system; and provided he is not conceited, and does not think that he is the man, and that wisdom shall die with him, he has a right to his system; and the Arminian thinks his way, the Calvinist his, and the Arian his. They have their schemes of the universe; but the trouble is that they are almost all pocket-schemes. Men's way of thinking is not God's way of thinking. "As the heavens are higher than the earth, so are my thoughts higher than your thoughts, saith the Lord." The difficulty with our systems of religion is that they are not big enough to comprehend all the knowledge and experience of the world. They are provincial, limited, narrow; and if you make them dogmatical and despotic they are cruel. Dogma is indispensable to religion, but it must be in its place.

There comes another man. He is not a reasoning nor a venerating man. He is one who believes in emotion. He likes a joyful hallelujah which well nigh takes the roof off. Occasions where there is singing, and shouting, and seizing by the hand, and laughing, and being happy, and making glad in religion—those suit him. "Ah! that is glory, that is glory;" he says. But do I revile that? No. I like to see it, provided a man does not say that that is the only thing in the universe. I say that in due measure it is to be respected instead of ridiculed.

Another man comes along and says, "Oh, the beauty of creation! Oh, the loveliness of virtue! How sweet are these sentiments!" Do I revile men of taste? Oh no, I do not revile them except when they attempt to despotize over me, and say to me, "My style of thinking is to be your style, or else you are a publican and sinner." Taste, in its time and proportion, is one element of religion. Religion is the whole of all these things.

Then comes a practical man, and he says, "You talk about your metaphysics and emotions and sentiments; but what I believe in is good square matter-of-fact common-sense ideas. Show me something to do, and I will do it. That is what I call being a Christian." Well, to my thinking, he is a dead man who has no thoughts and feelings and sentiments. You can grind out, with Babbage's calculating machine, results about as good as these pragmatical men produce. Matter-of-fact things are good; but they are infinitely better where they are accompanied by taste and reason and veneration and beneficence than where they are without these accompaniments; for the whole is better than any single element. And all of these elements may be abundantly found.

Look at the ethical feeling—that is, the sense of duty and fidelity and right. See how strong it is, the world over. Take the element of humanity. Was there ever a time when the whole world's heart throbbed as it does to-day in response to calls for help that come from the needy? Let Chicago be burned, and, before the last peal of the alarm bells has sounded, from London thousands and hundreds of thousands of dollars are coming in. Let there be famine in India, and American Christians instantly send ships thither laden with supplies. Let disease sweep New Orleans, and every village or hamlet in New England takes steps for its relief. And do you tell me that humanity is growing less? It never was so broad and high and deep as it is to-day.

Take the element of domestic virtue. There never was a time when the household lived on so high a plane. There never was a time when "father" seemed so venerable, or when "mother" was such a charm to bring the thought of heaven to the soul. There never was a time when so many men were homesick for home. There never was a time when so many looked back upon the family in which they were brought up as a Garden of Eden from which they have been expelled by age and duty. The household was never before so much a power as it is now. It is subject to assaults, open or covert, but it will dash all these things from it. As the human body has in it a resiliency, or repellant power, by which it throws off morbific influences and attacks, so the household has a power of virtue which never was so radiant and so irresistible as it is to-day. When the foundations of the family are adamantine, and when there is a crystal dome extending over it through which men see God and heaven, tell me not that religion is in danger. The family is God's primal church; and to-day it is the nearest like the divine and heavenly state of all things that we have.

Public spirit, which is a form of beneficence, was never stronger than it is to-day. It is growing more and more universal. And I judge of the preaching of a place by the public spirit which I see exhibited there. If I go through a village and see that the town pump is in a dilapidated condition, and the fences are tumbling down, and the town house is a rattlety-bang affair, taken possession of more by winds and rains than by men, and that the churches are poor, and the almshouse is a miserable place, and the roads are stony, and that there are no bridges but rails with a few clods thrown on them,—I say, "There is poor doctrine preached in this village." For any true preaching of religion will make men public spirited. No man can be preached to as he ought to be in regard to his duty to God and men without his religion having a reflex influence on his house, his barn, the public highways, everything that belongs to him in common with his fellow men. "Ye are brethren" is a part of the Gospel. Religion is not love to God alone: it is love to man as well. Among other things, it means public spirit—and by that test I think there is not a good gospel preached in some parts of New Hampshire!

Democracy in its true sense belongs to religion. Religion extends its walls about everything in creation. It looks upon all men, whether they be ignorant or educated, high or low, good or bad, as one household. It has that spirit which leads a man to extend warm quickening sympathies to his fellow men in proportion as they need them. Religion, where it exists in its highest form among men, draws them to those who are bad quicker than to those who are good, that they may give them help and succor.

This spirit is spreading everywhere; and I do not despair

of seeing the time when in even heathen nations the true spirit of reflected Christianity shall have its influence, and when men can go around and around the globe and find in every tribe and section—in the wilderness and everywhere—the common feeling that man is a child of God, and goes back to God, and is immortal.

That is not all. I ask you to consider what religion is according to the definition of Paul:

"The fruit of the Spirit is love, peace, long-suffering, gentleness, goodness, faith, meekness, temperance."

A man, going down to Boston, hears of Cushing's place. Everybody, I suppose, who has been to Boston, has heard of that place. There are magnificent flowers, and all sorts of fruits there. The fruits are the world's wonder for variety and lusciousness and perfectness. This man drives out to Cushing's, and goes around the place. When he gets there, the first thing he looks at is the fence; and he says, "Well, this place is not what it is cracked up to be—look at that fence! I have a better fence than that about my lot at home." He goes into the grounds and looks at the lawns, shaven and shorn, and he says, "I'd give more for my old medder with timothy hay in it than this docked, shaved lawn." He looks at the house, and says, "I thought it would be a fine castle, but it is only a house." He goes into the orchard and looks at the fruit-trees, and says, "There is a great deal of bad bark on those trees." But he came to see the fruit; and what has the fence, or the lawn, or the house, or the bark on the trees to do with that? The way to judge of the value of the orchard, or garden, or grapery, or hot-house is to try the fruit. The test of the fruit is the fruit itself. If the apples, and the pears, and the plums, and the peaches, and the grapes, and the figs, and what not, are good, that is enough. If they are large and ripe and luscious, what more can he ask? I do not care whether a man whitewashes or blackwashes his fence, or whether he uses guano or barn-yard manure, or what his mode of cultivation may be, the question is, Does he get good fruit? If he does, his method is good.

Now, I take it that the apostle is speaking of religion

when he speaks of the fruit of the Spirit; and the fruit of the Spirit is what? Orthodoxy? Oh, no. Conscience? Not a bit of it. One of the fruits of the Spirit is love; and is love dead? Does it no longer rock the cradle? Does it no longer sit patiently through the day and night by the bed of pain and sickness? Does it weep no longer for the outcast wanderer? Is there no sacrifice that love makes?

Another fruit of the Spirit is joy; and is joy gone? Is there no merriment among children? Are there no longer hours of conscious fidelity and heroism? Are there no acts, are there no developments, which imply the exercise of the noblest parts in men? Are they shaking down no fragrant dews in the soul? Is joy like a worn-out instrument whose strings are broken and whose body is smashed? Is joy voiceless and tuneless? Was the world ever before so full of joy as to-day?

Peace, the strangest of fruits—is it not slowly coming to be that which is the unison of all other qualities with blessedness in the soul? I do not mean that peace which is lethargic and sacrifices nothing, but that peace which comes from the excitement of all parts of our nature, carrying them above the ordinary line of experience. It is high up that the most perfect peace is. There are places in the nooks and ravines of the mountains where there is peace; but they who go up in balloons say that as they rise above the earth all sounds die away, and that high up in the pure ether there is perfect silence. And so, as men rise through the experience and trials of life, they find that high up there is a realm of peace. Is peace dying?

Some tell me they do not believe in religion because of the way that men act in Wall street; because they see elders, and deacons, and ministers even, doing wrong things. Of course they do wrong. They would not be in the human body if they did not. But go and see what mothers bear for sons. Go and see, in miniature, that same atoning sacrifice which Christ fulfilled, in those who literally give their life, living it, giving it, for the unworthy, the poor and the needy. Do you tell me that religion is dying out? It blossoms everywhere. Every household is full of it. Every village is filled with it. Orthodoxy, the exact statement of things, may be shattered; church order may be changed; but never will religion die out until the human soul is void of love, joy, peace, long-suffering, goodness, faith, meekness, and temperance.

Ye, then, who mourn because particular modes are changing, and think that religion is dying out, look deeper, and pluck up hope out of your despair, and confidence out of your fear. And to you that think religion is going away because of science, let me say that science is the handmaid of religion; it is the John Baptist, oftentimes, that clears the way for true religion. By religion I do not mean outward things, but inward states. I mean perfected manhood. I mean the quickening of the soul by the beatific influence of the divine Spirit in truth, and love, and sympathy, and confidence, and trust. That is not dying out. Not until the soul of man is quenched can religion die out. Not until God ceases to be God can religion be quenched in this world. It may have its nights and days; it may have its winter and summer; it may be subject to the great laws of oscillation and change; but, nevertheless, the word of God standeth sure; its foundations are immutable; and not until the last generation has been born and translated, not until the last tear has been shed, not until the last pulse of love has throbbed, not until the new heavens and the new earth appear, will religion die on the earth or lose its power among men.

PRAYER BEFORE THE SERMON.

We rejoice, our Father, that our thoughts are lifted, not by our wills alone, but by the inspiration of God; for we cannot discern the things that are spiritual and afar off save by divine help. Thou that broodest the world, and dost spread abroad thy wings and it is night, and let thy face shine and it is day—thou everywhere the beloved and the loving, we rejoice in thy succor and inspiration and help; and we implore thee, this morning, not because thou needest imploration, but because it is sweet for us to ask, and to behold that the blessings which we ask are given graciously. We draw near to thee as our children to us, that draw near with their helplessness and with their wants. We desire to draw near to thee with their confiding faith, and their love unaffected. We call thee our Father. Thou hast made thyself known to us as such. We do not discern in thee dreadful power, nor do we discern in thee the scowl of oppression and of cruelty. Our thought of thee is of all truth, of all justice and equity, of all gentleness and sympathy, of all love and helpfulness. What our father and our mother were to us, that art thou ten thousand times ten thousand fold. We grope as in the dark. We are like tapers here. Thou art the sun rolling in the immensity of thy being, and giving light and warmth to every one. We are afraid, O Lord our God, often, to trust in thee, fearing to exhaust thy mercy, which is ineffable, universal and inexhaustible. Thou dost pity us, knowing our frame, and remembering that we are dust. Thou dost succor the ill-deserving, causing thy sun to rise upon the good and the bad, sending rain upon the just and upon the unjust, and filling the earth with thy bounty so that all creatures, not excepting those that are seemingly most worthless, are still cared for. The insect of the air, the worm of the earth, the fish of the sea, the cattle upon a thousand hills, all things that are created, are objects of thy thought. Thou dost watch over them; and how much more is man, made in thine image, destined to draw near unto thee, and to become a son of God in the heavenly land, perfected. In thee is our hope. Not in ourselves, but in the greatness, in the mercy, in the grace, and in the everlasting bounty of our God, we find inspiration of hope and of trust; for thou dost shelter those that know how to come underneath the shadow of thy wings. Thou art the tower to which, when hard pressed, thy people run, and are saved from their pursuers. Thou art the shadow of a great rock in a weary land; and blessed are they that know how to sit down in the shade in the midst of surrounding heat. We desire, O Lord our God, that thy name may shine more clearly, and that thy heart may be more aboundingly known among thine own people, and that those who are children may become witnesses more worthy of their parentage, and have more of joy and strength and faith and patience ministered unto them through the might and goodness of their God.

Vouchsafe thy blessing to rest upon us now, in the hour in which we are gathered together. How many of us! From what diverse ways! From what different experiences! And yet all united together by common infirmity, by common sinfulness, by a common need of forgiveness, and by a common necessity for that love which comes only from the soul of God.

Vouchsafe to each one in thy presence, this morning, that which each one needs. Search the hidden grief of every one, and either heal it or give grace to bear it. Be with those that are near to thee in supplication day by day, and that will not let thee go without the blessing longed for, more precious to them than life itself. Hear their prayers, and answer them.

Those that carry sorrows, and wear them as a garment all the year round, and are acquainted with grief—vouchsafe thy presence, likewise, this day to them; and may they hear inwardly their name called of thee, even as Mary, in the midst of her tears, was called by her name by our Lord and Saviour.

And we beseech of thee that thou wilt strengthen the weak, and succor those that are in peril through overmastering temptations. Deliver from evil those that are beginning to be drawn into its whirl. We beseech thee that thou wilt look piteously upon every want and every necessity. May those that hunger and thirst after righteousness more and more be fed and filled. May those that are drawing near to the confines of life rejoice and look away to that eternal youth beyond, which waits for them. May those that are in the midst of life fulfill their duties with a right manly sincerity and earnestness. May those that are young grow up uncontaminated. With truth and honor and manhood undefiled may they enter into the places of those that are departing, and do better than their fathers have done. We beseech of thee that thou wilt grant thy blessing to rest upon all our friends that are separated from us. Go with us homeward. Lead us to our children and our children's children, to our companions, to our parents, to our brothers and sisters, far away across the seas, in the wilderness, everywhere; and unite us in that love which is upon them and upon us at the same time.

We beseech thee that thou wilt grant thy blessing to rest upon this house and household; upon those that abide here and minister to our comfort; upon all that are gathered here to spend the days of vacation; and grant that this house may be filled with peace and joy. May everything that is benign and pure rule over whatever is selfish and proud and hateful. May the spirit of joy and of gladness, springing from sincerity and purity, prevail here from hour to hour, so that the blessing of the Lord shall dwell upon this place forever more.

We commend ourselves to thee. Take care of us while we live. Mark our years out for us. Not for our asking give us more or less, but according to thy wisdom. Think for us, dear Lord; ordain for us; and then make us able to say, in every emergency, The will of the Lord be done; till we have passed the vail, and the shadows flee, and the morning comes. Arise, O Sun of Righteousness, with healing in thy beams, and bring us where there is no night and no more sorrow forever. *Amen.*

PRAYER AFTER THE SERMON.

QUICKEN our faith, Almighty God. O thou Saviour that hast loved us, and loved us in our weakness and want, and art loving us into strength, and into truth, and into justice, and into patience, and into godliness, love us still. This is a wonder that we never could interpret if we had not been parents ourselves. See how we love our children, though they be erring. Others do not love them in their weakness, but we do; and thou lookest out of a larger heart of the same kind as ours. But while thou knowest how to teach the lore of love, thou knowest how to lay upon men responsibility; for whom thou lovest thou chastenest, and scourgest every son whom thou receivest. May we, then, have more and more confidence in thee, and accept the duties and discipline of life with more gratitude and cheerfulness and hopefulness, looking forward; for we are not to stay a great while here. We are in tabernacles. The city that hath foundations is not far off. We hear the voices of its inhabitants. From off the walls come wafted to us, now and then, the word of cheer, *Come;* and he that hears repeats it, and says Come; and whosoever will, let him come. And all are coming. All find their way back toward the Sun of Righteousness.

Grant, O Lord our God, that we may have more faith in thee, more hope for the world, more sympathy for the race, more kindness toward each other, so that we may stand holding each other up, pitying each other's faults, helping those that are cast down, and doing most for those that are most needy. May we seek out those that are in sorrows, and minister to them. Make us like thyself, thou that didst give thy life, laying it down and taking it up again, and that art forever, in heavenly places, carrying thy life, not for thyself, but for others; and being made like thee, may we be called sons of God, and find rest with thee in the heavenly land. We ask it through riches of grace in Christ Jesus. *Amen.*

II.

CHRISTIAN SYMPATHY.

CHRISTIAN SYMPATHY.

"For as we have many members in one body, and all members have not the same office; so we, being many, are one body in Christ, and every one members one of another."—ROM. xii. 4, 5.

Is this sympathetic unity a peculiarity of church life? Are these words meant to explain simply that when a great number of persons are joined in a church connection they are in a spiritual, sympathetic unity? Yes, it means that, on the way to something a great deal larger than that. It is the declaration—and the spirit of it runs through the New Testament, and colors every part of it—it is the declaration that the ideal condition of the human race is one in which mankind are knit together by a sympathy which makes one man the brother of another man, the world over; and that too, as is explained by the Apostle Paul in 1st Corinthians, the 12th chapter, without regard to nationality, or sect, or condition in life—whether bond or free, Jew or Gentile, in the church or out of the church. The ideal condition, or that condition toward which God's providence is steadily conducting the races of the world, and which they will reach when they shall be ripe, is a condition in which every man shall feel that every other man is a part of himself; or, in other words, in which every man shall feel as a parent feels in the family, that every other person is in one sense a part of himself. Mankind will yet come—they are not in a hurry, but they will come—to that condition in which nothing will be so

Preached at the TWIN MOUNTAIN HOUSE, White Mountains, N. H., Sunday morning, August 30th, 1874. Lesson: Rom. xii. Hymns (Plymouth Collection): Nos. 102, 632.

near to the heart of man as *man*, without regard to the fact of relationship, kindred, interest, or neighborhood. The time is approaching when the mere fact that one is a human being will open and kindle the hearts of men toward him in all sympathy and kindness.

It is of this unity, which springs from the Gospel—the sympathetic unity of soul with soul—that I shall speak this morning.

I have said that this was not a matter of the artificial life of the church; and let me say that I look upon the church, not as a substitute for anything, but simply as an instrument, as an educating institution, by which God attempts to diffuse the light and knowledge of true manhood throughout the race. It is a subservient institution. It is not itself a primary thing. It is secondary. In the work of ages the church is full of grandeur and excellence; yet it is simply subordinate, doing the Master's will.

God's heart and God's purpose are the salvation of the world; and it is the deliverance, the elevation of every living human being on the globe, that lies before the divine mind as the reason and motive of administration through the periods of time; and the church bears relation to this great end just as the common school bears relation to the prevalence of intelligence through the community. We believe in schools and academies; but we value the community more than we do even them. Their worth lies in the fact that they are blessing the whole community. They are not in themselves sacred; they are not valuable except for such worthy objects as they may serve; they are good for what they do: and the church is good for only that which it accomplishes. What is greater than any church is that for which the church was created—namely, universal mankind.

We are therefore to suppose, not that God is working for the Jew or for the Gentile, for the Asiatic or for the African, for the European or for the American, but for all of them.

We are not to suppose that the divine providence is watching alone over good people, virtuous people, healthy people; it watches over all alike. It makes the sun to rise on the evil and on the good, and sends rain on the just and on the unjust. The divine purposes have respect to every one, everywhere, without regard to nationality or condition.

Such is the ideal state. It is one toward which the feelings of sympathy, of benevolence, and of love, man for man, are perpetually tending.

So, when we speak of the unity which all mankind are seeking, we shall not be able to form a just opinion respecting it unless we take into consideration this internal unity. Everybody wants unity in the churches, everybody is striving to bring them together; and there would be no difficulty in uniting them outwardly if that were enough; but what would be the advantage of a mere external unity of the churches?

What advantage would it be in a village if all the inhabitants should say, "The citizens of this village should be perfectly united; and, therefore, let us move our houses up so that they will touch each other. Moreover, let all the people of this town have the one name, *Adams*. Let them all call themselves, and be called, by that name. Besides, let us all have breakfast and dinner and supper at the same hour and minute, at the stroke of the bell." They might secure unity in these outward things, so as to be able to say, "There is not such a united village in the world as we are;" but what would be the advantage of mere external unity in a village? Suppose every village in the land should march in such a unity, as soldiers march on a parade, would they be any better or happier? Physical, material unity may flatter pride, perhaps, and give argument for boasting; but it will not raise a man one step in the scale of intelligence, or make him kinder, or destroy his prejudices. It will not make the cruel man lenient, nor the impatient man long-suffering, nor the despotic man merciful. It will do no good.

But the churches have been calling to each other for unity. The Presbyterian church is going to have one church throughout the world when the kingdom of Christ comes; and that one church is going to be a Presbyterian church. The Episcopalian church is going to have one great church; and that great church is going to eat up all the little churches; and it is going to be an Episcopal church. The same is true of the Baptist and Methodist churches. But the Congregationalists believe in none of these hierarchies; they believe that each of them has some elements of truth, and that when the millennium comes, that which is good in all of them will be gathered up and brought together; and this means that all Christendom is going to be Congregational!

But the church a man is in is much like the clothes he wears, provided he is fitted. I wear black, and some of you wear blue. Some of you wear short coats, and some long. Some wear one kind of hat, and some another. It is not the hat, not the coat, nor anything of the kind, that we think about in judging of a man's character; and the fact that there are different denominations or sects is of little account if only they behave themselves, and do not quarrel, and are peaceable, and are not arrogant, and do not pretend that they are the one people who know God's secrets, and do not claim to be ordained to rule over their fellow-men, and do not sit on their peculiar throne of creed or church and say to all others, "Bow down to us when you hear our sackbut and psaltery, or we will burn you up." The trouble is, not that there are so many sects, but that they are often weak in that which is good, and strong in that which is bad.

It is not, therefore, organic unity, nor unity of belief exactly, that we are seeking. I never saw a man who was large enough to report the whole truth in respect to anything which he looked at. It has not been considered safe, I think, in heaven, where the manufactory of men is, to put everything in everybody. The result is, that one man carries so much, another man so much, and another man so much. Why, it takes about twenty men to make one sound man. One man is hopeful and impetuous; another is cautious and slow; and the two put together would make a much more evenly balanced man than either of them is separately. One man is reflective; another is perceptive; and the two united would make a better man than either of them alone. One man looks at things as an enthusiast; another sees things in a matter-of-fact light; and if the two were put together they would temper each other. And when fifteen or twenty men come together, and accept the truth as it is seen by all of them combined, they have a far more comprehensive knowledge of it than they would have if they only saw it from their individual standpoints. When each one has made his statement of it, and infused into it all the elements that are in him, they will be nearer to a full presentation of it than any one of them could come simply by his understanding of it.

Men want unity of belief; but I would like to know how they are going to have it so long as they are made to differ as they do now. For instance, here is a man of enormous self-esteem. Firmness stands like an adamantine column in his disposition. He sees everything in the light of duty and law. He says, "It is the business of men to obey the law;" and he sympathizes with the magistrate. Says he, "If men have sinned they ought to be punished; the law was made to punish sinners"—and he would like to be the man to carry it out. He is, every particle of him, in sympathy with government and law.

Take another man. He has enormous benevolence; he has not much self-esteem; and he sympathizes with *men* instead of laws. He sees everything in its relations to the poor and suffering and needy.

One of these men will say, "The law is broken, and penalty must follow." The other will say, "Oh, poor transgressors! what will become of them?"

How are you going to make men who are organized so differently read the Bible and see everything alike? When you read the Bible you will see one thing, and when another reads the Bible he will see another thing, owing to the differences of your organizations.

If you mix on a plate iron filings, pieces of flint, a little Indian meal, and a little flour, and take a magnet, and draw it through, it will not touch the meal nor the flour nor the flint, but it will pick up all the iron filings.

Now, men are magnets, and if you draw them through the Bible they will catch the things which they are sensitive to, while they will pass by the things which they are not sensitive to. Proud, domineering men will catch the elements which tend toward government. Kind, generous, democratic people will catch the elements that tend toward kindness and generosity and democracy. Men who are characterized by taste will catch the elements of taste. Those of imagination will catch poetic elements. Each one will catch those elements which are peculiar to himself.

How, then, are you going to take men as they are made, and make them believe alike? Some persons are so dry that you might soak them in a joke for a month, and it would not go through their skin. No explanation would suffice to make them understand it. They must accept it by faith if they accept it at all. And yet, there are other persons who are so sensitive to everything that is humorous or ludicrous that probably there is not a thing on earth that does not, first or last, suggest something funny to them. How are you going to take such minds, and make them look along the track of truth and see alike? They are made differently, and it is not without a purpose. For variety—organized variety—is strength. A community is strong by the differences and not by the likenesses that exist in it.

Suppose every man in a town were a blacksmith, and nothing else! Fortunately it is never so. Among the people in a town, some are tinners, some are hatters, some are weavers, some are carpenters, some are painters, some are merchants, and some are bankers. The town is rich by the variety of its trades and callings.

Now, in beliefs there are certain great stable, fundamental facts which nobody doubts; as, for instance, that of sunrise or sunset. We all believe in the revolution of the globe. All men agree in regard to certain fixed truths in mathematics. There is no great schism in the matter of arithmetic; everybody acknowledges that two and two make four. But when you come to questions which involve feeling, probably no two persons agree at all. If you could sharply look in and see just how the same proposition strikes two persons, you would probably find that if it was a proposition where emotion was concerned they would not agree. It is colored in one, perhaps, by imagination, which is predominant in him, and in the other by a predominating reflective reason. One person is cautious and hesitant, and another is headlong and venturesome, and these facts make it impossible for them to view the same truth in the same light. One man is remarkable for coolness, and another for intensity of feeling; and they will differ in their impressions of a truth according to their individualisms.

These things being so, how preposterous it is for any church to undertake to give a solution of the nature of God, which involves every conceivable question of human disposition! We can know God only so far as we have sparks of him in ourselves. To delineate the whole history of divine providence for thousands of years; to explain the various questions of moral government which arise; to determine the various methods and doctrines of responsibility and penalty and reward; to unfold the whole theory of the human mind; to undertake encyclopediacal knowledge, running through the whole career of the race—how shall this be done so that everybody shall see everything just exactly alike? It is absolutely impossible. God laughs when he sees fool Man trying to do it. It is against nature. So, all the strifes and quarrels of the different sects, to bring everybody to see things just as they see them, are waste work. It never will be done.

Well, as you cannot have external and organic unity, nor an exact unity of beliefs, from the very structure of the human mind, there seems to be but one other kind of unity that you can come to; and that is the unity of the Spirit in the bond of perfectness, or sympathetic unity.

Come, go with me into a house where there is father, where there is mother, where there are eight children, where there are two servants, and where there are three or four friends. They are all of one church; they are all of one business; they all live under one roof; they all either are of one name, or are very nearly associated in name; and you say, "They are at perfect unity." No, they are not; they quarrel like cats and dogs. It is an unhappy household. They have all the unity that the church is striving after; but it does them no good.

Go with me into another house. There are father and mother, and eight children, and two or three friends; and they are sweet-tempered, genial and kind; but they belong to very different churches. They are gathered together from various quarters; but they all happen to be alike in loving each other. They think differently and believe differently, but that does not prevent their being united. Difference is perfectly compatible with unity. For, are there not four parts to a good tune? and do not all these parts help each other? Differences are only methods of unity, provided they are concordant.

In the great family here at this [Twin Mountain] house there is more unity to-day than there is at large in any church or sect in Christendom. You have come together from every direction; there are hardly any two of you of the same name; you are crowded into this room under circumstances of very great inconvenience; and yet you are polite one to another. You are willing that all others should have seats (—after you are provided for!) There is no strife here. You are harmonious. You wish well to each other. You are even kindly disposed to believe what I say. And yet you are from different churches. You belong to sects of almost every name; but still, there is a genial, kind sympathy existing between you. In short, you are gentlemen and ladies—for the time being! Everything moves in unison. And I will venture to say that there is not a room in this house where there will not be greater happiness after this service. I will venture to say that you will feel kinder to each other, and nearer to each other, and more helpful of each other, during this week for the experience of this morning; it is the natural result of a season of united feelings. And I ask you if such unity is not the best kind. I ask you if inward, sympathetic, benevolent unity is not the unity that does good.

This, then, is the dominant Christian idea of oneness—namely, unity of the heart. A man who is royally endowed with bodily and mental gifts, and who holds himself in such a sweet alliance with every human being that he carries himself genially and helpfully toward all, is a true Christian. Of course such a man carries himself so toward those that he loves as his own; but let a man who is blessed with a superior intellect, with rare physical endowments, and with circumstances favorable to their development and use, carry himself in a spirit of kindness and gentleness toward the poorest, the lowest and the meanest, and he represents the ideal of Christian manhood. When a man comes to that high state he is Christ's, not only, but he exhibits Christ to men. When the church comes to that state it instantly becomes the true catholic church—that is to say, it becomes the church which is going to take possession of the world—the church of the heart, the church of sympathy, the church of benevolence, the church of love.

By this spirit of sympathy one with another, I remark first, all hatreds, and all injurious conduct under different names of pretension, are forbidden. We have no right to inflict pain except as a physician administers bitter medicines. We have no right to make men suffer except as a surgeon amputates a limb. We have no right to resort to penalties except as the schoolmaster punishes his pupils. We may inflict pain and cause suffering and resort to penalties so far as they are necessary to prevent the repetition of evil in an individual, or to prevent others from experiencing them, under which circumstances they are not cruel. No human being has a right to cause any form of injury except for a benevolent purpose. The doctrines that teach that God's administration in the world is one of vengeance, and that it is continued for no other reason than because God chooses to perpetuate it, make God a demon, and not a Father. All pains and penalties are to be beneficent, and they are to be administered beneficently. A judge has no right to judge a man with a cold, unsympathizing heart. A father has no right to punish a child with an unfeeling, angry spirit. No man has a right to mulct his neighbor, or inflict suffering upon him in any way, except for his good. No man knows what justice is who does not know what love is. There is no justice except the equity that moves under the influence of love. This is the Christian doctrine. All other doctrines are anti-Christian.

Secondly, this spirit of universal sympathy, this spirit of brotherhood between man and man, forbids envy and jealousy of every kind. You perhaps do not believe that there are such things as envy and jealousy; but if these qualities could only squeak like unoiled hinges, there would be such a noise in every community that you would think Bedlam had been let loose. Envies and jealousies do not generally go out except in masquerade. They put on various masks and disguises of society—philosophic statements and the like; but back of these all their hateful features are to be seen. The community is full of persons who are unhappy because other persons are better off than they. One man gets what another man coveted; and the latter says, "There! he has got the property that is mine—that is, that I wanted." The rich and the poor look with jealousy upon each other. The poor are angry because the rich get so much while they get so little; and the rich are angry because the poor are in the way of their getting more. Competitors in politics or merchandise look at each other with the lower and smaller forms of petty envy and jealousy.

But, the word of God says, "In honor preferring one another." It enjoins upon us the duty of giving the preference to others. Does anybody really do this? Yes! I should like to know if the mother, when she sits down to the table with her children, picks out the best things, and eats them, and gives the children what is left. Does not she in love prefer every child? And, going down, she is more attentive to the youngest than to those that are older. She does not disown the twenty-one-year-old boy, nor the sixteen-year-old, nor the twelve-year-old; but, after all, the little babe in the cradle rules the whole of them. Her sensibility and kindness increase in the ratio of their need.

Now, that which the mother feels is the type of universal motherhood, or the true Christian feeling when it shall have been ripened in human nature. Every man is to come into that state in which he shall feel for others kindness and goodwill, so that their prosperity shall be his joy, and so that if he puts out his hand for some promised fruit, and another, quicker than he, gets it, he shall draw back his hand and say, "Thank God, it is yours. I am glad that you got it." That is not the way that men do now-a-days generally; but it is the Christian way.

In politics men do not prefer one another. They strive by every means to prevent the community from preferring others. Men are standing on the ground of selfish animalism. Society is organized on the same principles of offense and defense which prevail among the beasts of the field. The law of strength and violence is a hundred times stronger in the world to-day, outsid· of the household, than the law of kindness and love and sympathy. But there is a day coming when the household feeling will become the neighborhood feeling, and the town feeling, and the county feeling, and the state feeling, and the national feeling. Then, when nation after nation comes into this higher manhood, and the public sentiment of the globe begins to be that of love and sympathy, the new heaven and the new earth in which dwelleth righteousness will have come.

We are far from that day. We see the dim morning twilight which foretokens it, but that is all; yet the day is coming when the animal in men will not predominate as it does now.

So the true spirit of the Christian man condemns indifference; and for the same reason that it condemns this it condemns all neglect, all carelessness. They are wrong. You have no right to be without feeling for others. It may be that your occupation is such that you are absent-minded; but no man ought to be in the presence of another person, though it be only a child, and a beggar's brat, without experiencing a feeling of interest in that person. Anything that has the stamp of humanity on it ought to excite in your bosom positive sympathy and good will.

It would be impossible for a man to walk in a gallery of magnificent pictures and not be affected by them, unless he was absent-minded; and it ought to be impossible for a man to walk among men and not have a genial, brotherly feeling toward them. Strangers come together, and not having been introduced they will walk past each other time and again, and never exchange a word. Men will ride together for hours in a stage-coach without any intercourse whatever; or if there is any, it will be of the most formal character, because they have not been introduced to each other.

Many men who are not church-members have more true

Christian spirit in them than many who are; for they do not go anywhere without feeling kindness, gentleness, good-humor, good-nature—and good-nature, if it is not a grace, is the nurse of all graces, that brings them up. The man who carries that with him everywhere and always is better than a man that is gruffly orthodox.

There are men who go about making everbody happy—and it does not take a great deal to make men happy, oftentimes. A little attention makes some people happy.

I recollect meeting in the street, in Brooklyn, one day, a carpenter who had made some repairs on my house. I stopped and said, "How do you do?" and shook hands with him. "Now," said he, "you big folks, who live in fine houses, do not know how much good it does a poor fellow when you speak to him and shake hands with him; but I tell you it does him a great deal of good. Why, your stopping and speaking to me, and shaking hands with me, will make me and my folks happy for a week. When I go home to-night my wife will say, 'Where have you been? and who have you seen?' and I will say, 'I have seen Mr. Beecher.' 'What did he say?' 'Oh, he shook hands with me, and asked after my family.' She will go on asking questions, and the children will ask questions, and we shall talk about it all the evening, and all the week, and it will make us all happy. It isn't much to you, but it is a good deal to us."

There is many a man in this audience who could make happiness follow him as phosphorescent light follows a ship's wake on the sea; but most of you are so genteel that you do not think it would be proper for you to have to do with others unless you have been introduced; and some of you say, "It is not for us to mix with the vulgar herd;" and others are timid and sensitive, and hesitate on that account. But there is not one of you that is not honored and beloved of God in the proportion in which you let your light shine so that other men may walk in the path which you make luminous.

Indifference to men is a sin. It is not necessary to your being a criminal that you should murder, or commit burglary, or set a house on fire, or pick some man's pocket. If you take your culture, and taste, and sensibility, and wrap yourself up in them, and walk alone among your fellow-men, touching nobody, kindling nobody, sympathizing with nobody, except one here and there whom you select as a companion for yourself, you are a criminal before God; and there is many a man that walks thus who is a greater sinner than the man who is hanged, for the law of Christian sympathy is absolute; it is the imperial law of the realm. It is the ideal of Christian life; and he who violates it by counting his fellow-men as nothing, as dust under his feet, as dirt, violates the fundamental law of the universe, and is a criminal.

We always sympathize to a certain extent. He is a bad man who does not sympathize with his own kin—though often you find men who do not do it. Not unfrequently you find that men who are benign on the street are ugly at home; and, quite as frequently, you find that men who are hard, and whose teeth are like knives in business, are very saints at home. You could not pry open their hand with a burglar's tool on the street; but when they go home it is broad open. They would not give anything outside of their household; but if their wife and children want anything they readily grant it. If you saw them at home and nowhere else you would say that they were princes of generosity; but if you saw them abroad and nowhere else you would say that they were tighter than the bark on growing trees. Now, we should expect a man to be in sympathy with those who bear his name and carry his blood; but that is not enough. "If ye love them that love you, what thank have ye?" "If ye salute your brethren only, what do ye more than others? Do not even the publicans the same?"

With our neighbors, also, we are apt to be in sympathy—provided it is not when we are in collision. For example, on a holiday, at a military muster, or on any occasion that brings the people together, there is generally a good-nature, a kindness of feeling, manifested by neighbors toward each other, which is not usual at other times and places. Men who at home, working on their farms or in their shops, do not care for their neighbors, when they get away from home, and meet them as persons that live near them, feel very much drawn toward them.

You will see that in traveling abroad. Men to whom in Brooklyn I used to say a simple "Good morning," in Paris, when I was home-sick, I wanted to put my arms about. They lived near where I lived, and that was under the circumstances a sufficient reason for my feeling drawn to them. It is a diffusive form of selfishness which leads you, when you are away from home, and see persons who live near where you do, to sympathize with them. People sympathize with their own households, with their neighbors, and with their own countrymen, as against foreigners.

Men having the same interests—as, for instance, stockholders in the same concern, if it is paying a good dividend —sympathize with each other. Selfishness sympathizes with selfishness, everywhere and always. We sympathize with persons of our own sect. We sympathize with them intensely when they are attacked by another sect, though not so intensely at other times. When nobody attacks us, we go to work to point out heresy among ourselves, and are like hounds pursuing each other. There never was a man on earth so orthodox but that there was somebody a little higher than he in orthodoxy who looked down upon him, and said, "You are not orthodox." There is always some one who thinks he is a little nearer to God than anybody else. The scale is infinitesimal; and when there is not a revival, or some other special influence to knit men together, those of the same denomination are apt to criticise each other if there is the difference of a hair between them. If a Methodist brother builds his fence three-quarters of an inch over the line on the land of another Methodist brother, that is enough to furnish a pretext for all manner of lawsuits and quarrels— unless there is a great religious awakening, or unless there is some squabble between some other denomination and the Methodists, in which case these two brethren join hands and fight the common enemy. Men that quarrel with each other on farming will unite their forces in a Presidential election, and shout, and grow red in the face, in contending for their favorite candidate or party. An attack on sectarians from the outside brings them together very quick and very close.

And that is carried further. Men outside of the church

having so good an example in the church, why should they not follow it? As sectarians herd with sectarians, as men in one church sympathize with each other as against those of another church, so you will find men in society at large limiting their sympathy and good-will very nearly to those of their own sort.

In speaking thus, I do not undertake to lay down an extravagant doctrine, and say that we have no right to like those that are of our sort: we have that right. If I love painting, I have a right to associate especially with those who love painting. If I love reading, I have a right to associate with those who love reading. If I am a mechanic, I have a right to associate with mechanics. If I am a lawyer or jurist, I have a right to associate with men of that profession. I have a right to associate with men who are interested in the same things that I am. There is certainly a propriety in your following the law of affinity and likeness and preference in selecting your associates; but I object to your whole manhood being absorbed in that way. I object to your taking those that you like, and refusing all others because they are not of your sect or set. I think it is a selfishness that God frowns upon, and one that hurts your soul.

That is exactly the point that is brought out in the parable of the Good Samaritan. A man went down from Jerusalem to Jericho, and fell among thieves, that stripped him of his raiment, and wounded him, and departed leaving him half dead. He lay as if he had been in Wall street. And when a certain priest came that way and beheld him, and saw by his look that he was not a priest, he walked on, saying to himself, "He is not of my set;" and he had no sympathy and no feeling of humanity for him. By and by there came down a Levite, and he looked on him, and said, "Poor fellow! he has been rather roughly used," and walked on the other side. There came also down a Samaritan (*Samaritan* was a name as detestable in the Jews' ears as in your ears *Abolitionist* was twenty years ago); and he went where he was, and bound up his wounds, pouring in oil and wine, and put him on his own beast, and took him to the tavern, and paid his bills in advance, and said to the host, "Take care of him; and if any exigencies arise which shall make his expenses more, I will repay thee." "Which of these three was neighbor to the man that fell among thieves?" asks the Master. Well, which was?

Thus, you take care of those that take care of you, and sympathize with those that sympathize with you, and that is right enough; but you neglect those that are not of your sect and set and sort, and that is wrong. It is wicked. Every human being has a right in you, and you have a right in every human being. On God's globe there is not a man—not even in the farthest China—who is not your brother. There is not a poor devotee on earth that bows down to river or star who is not your brother or sister. The whole human family is one, of whom God is the Father. The blood of Jesus Christ is stronger than the blood of any earthly father or mother; and you are united by the blood of Christ into one great household.

Look at the repugnances which spring up among men, and judge them according to this law which I have been developing.

In the first place, we feel ourselves justified in having great indignation and great vindictiveness of feeling toward those who have by crime or vice forfeited their place and their citizens' right in society. I think the horror with which we teach our children to look upon thieves and burglars and harlots is one of the most pitiful of possible commentaries on human nature. I do not know that it is yet possible to bring to bear upon the criminal classes influences which shall wholly restrain them without resorting to the employment of physical force and the infliction of pain; but judged by this higher ideal, what a state of things it is in which, when men need most, and are dying for the want of somebody to look after them, and take care of them, and bear with them, because they are sinful, there is not in the community a church, hardly an individual, that knows how to suffer for the outcast as Jesus Christ suffered for the whole world! Christ died for his enemies, we are told. It is made conspicuous by every form of statement in the New Testament that God so loved the world that he gave his only begotten Son to die for it, while it was afar off from him, utterly unlike him, and repugnant to every conception of infinite purity and goodness. God's nature was such that he bowed down to succor and to save his creatures; and when he rose from the dead he lifted the world on his shoulders; yet in our own communities, at this late period of Christian teaching, we are brought up to abhor jailbirds as we do toads, and to detest vicious and criminal men as if they were snakes and vipers; and we shut them out of our hearts as if they were not men.

Now, as I hold, we must abhor vice and crime, and all that is evil; we must not introduce into our household economy those who shall pervert and destroy the purity of our children; we cannot be too careful on that side; and yet there is no man so cruel that his cruelty is not a plea to our compassion; and there is not a man so dishonest that his dishonesty is not a plea to our thoughtfulness and sympathy. If the Spirit of Christ were in us, we should desire to succor most those who most need succor. No man is so much in peril as the man whose passions are corrupted; and yet we tread down the criminal classes. But all such—the multitudes of vicious boys that run riot at night in our great cities; the great mass of feculent sediment that infests our streets; the thousands and hundreds of thousands that shock our taste and are repellent to our unsanctified natures—somebody must care for them or they will perish. God, methinks, the purest and the highest, is the only one that calls them brethren while we gather our garments up and walk on the other side, and leave them weltering in their vices.

All who are by disposition unlovely we feel justified in turning our backs upon. We think we have a right to eschew their company and speak evil of them. Here is a man that is hard and grasping; the whole neighborhood agree to call him an old hunks, an avaricious dog; and from the moment that is done, every thought we have about this man is one that strikes him. We do not pity him. We do not consider measures for his relief. We do not take remedial steps in respect to him.

Let a man come to this hotel, and let it be said of him, "Do you see that man? He was the guardian of an estate that was left to a family of children, and he cheated them out of it; he has their property; they are poor, and he is here spending their money." That would be infamous, I admit; but it would not justify me in treating him as if he were not a man. It would not be a reason why I should not preach to him and pray for him (for we are commanded to pray even for those who despitefully use us). He would not be out of the sphere of my sympathy because he was a wicked man. If you are a Christian, you ought to be in sympathy with men in the proportion in which they are wicked.

We cite the faults and foibles of men as reasons why we do not want to have anything to do with them; and we submit them, often, to the raillery of the community.

A man is constitutionally vain, but carries himself with constant awkwardness, and does not know it perhaps; and the young people whisper, and tell everything that they know about him, and ridicule him.

All churches talk about each other. And in politics and business men talk about each other. There is no Christianity of any conspicuous eminence that teaches us to bear each other's burdens. There is no Christianity that is very current which teaches us to sympathize with men because they are imperfect, or to take care of them because they have faults. There is no Christianity of any great prominence which teaches us to look after people's hearts on the same principle that we look after their bodies.

We feel, also, that we have a right to toss the head about poor, ignorant, shiftless men, who do not succeed in life. Men say, "Are you going to give anything more to that miserable creature? You might just as well pour water into a sieve. You might as well put money in a bag with holes in it. Why, he is one of the poorest, laziest, most shiftless wretches in the world." I understand perfectly well that there is a political economy, and that it is not best to adopt a system that will put a premium on laziness or shiftlessness; but do you know that laziness and shiftlessness are inborn? Do you know that if you are smart you got your smartness from father, or mother, or both, by lineal descent? Many persons are born without much will, and with very little force; they have a small stomach, no bigger than my hand; and when they throw down food into it, it is like a mill which has not much power to grind; and the blood that is made there is poor; and there is but little of it; the consequence is that when it is pumped up into the brain, having been very poorly aërated, it does not stimulate the faculties a great deal; it is pretty cold business that is carried on up there; and when it goes down again, and around, it goes sluggishly; and when it returns to the brain there is not as much electricity and snap and fire there in a whole day as you get in one single throb; and yet you stand, with your superior endowment, over against that poorly-endowed, badly-born man, who never had even any education as a compensation for his bad birth, and say, "Poor devil! let him alone. The best thing he can do is to die." That may be; but it is not very amiable for you to put him out of the pale of sympathy and succor simply because he needs so much.

I do not blame you so severely because you have been so badly brought up. You have been studying catechisms and creeds so that you have had no time to study conduct. You have been so busy thinking about church machinery that you have not had much time to think about Christian spirit and life. You have studied the body until you have forgotten that there is such a thing as the soul, or until you act as though you had. I do not blame you altogether—I pity you. If there is anybody that needs pity it is a man in a Christian community who does not know how to love as Christ loves. Men sometimes pin a red or blue rag on their shoulder as a badge to show what organization they belong to; and many professed Christians are known as such only by the rag of doctrine which they wear; but if any man have not the spirit of Christ he is none of his. Was there a harlot in all Galilee that could look upon Christ and he not know it, and speak peaceable things to her? And did he not abhor immorality? Did not thefts, and whoredoms, and all forms of iniquity rise before him blacker than they can rise before the human imagination? and yet, so much wickeder was it to be selfish with the intellect and the moral feelings than to be selfish with the passions, that he turned and looked upon the Pharisee and said, "The publicans and the harlots shall go into the kingdom of God before you." It is a solemn warning.

We talk about civilization and Christianity in the world; but when I see how men live; when I see how much the malign passions rule and how little they are subdued, I feel that there is a great deal lacking of that which constitutes true civilization and Christianity among men in the community at large; and I ask, "Where is beneficence? Is benevolence a real vital principle? Is everybody happier where you go? Does summer shine out of your soul and make summer for others?" I do not care for your churches and doctrines if they do not create in you the fruit of the Gospel. Without love to God and men your professions are vain and empty.

Now, I ask you whether there is not a difference between the natural man and the spiritual man. The common man is good-natured when everything pleases him. He has a sort of generous feeling when he has more than he knows what to do with. Under such circumstances he does not mind throwing out five dollars here and there, once in a while. He feels about money as I do about dirt. I do not value dirt very highly; and if a man wants a handful of dirt I will give it to him. I will not be stingy about it. Men are very generous when they begin to have a good deal; but when they get rich they are apt to become penurious, and to be suspicious in every way.

As it is with common men, so it is with Christians. When I see a man going about the community and prating about Christianity, I say to him, "Where is the radical principle of the Gospel—love? I do not care what church you are in. If you live in the spirit of the Lord Jesus Christ you are in the true church, no matter what the name of the external church to which you belong may be. If your spirit is one of kindness always and everywhere, you are right, no matter what teaching you have been under. The spirit of essential self-sacrifice and disinterested love is Christian, and nothing is Christian which comes short of that. In proportion as that spirit grows in you are you growing in grace, and orthodox; but in proportion as you substitute outward conformities for that spirit you are becoming heterodox, and going back to the world."

Oh, my friends, it is ineffably sweeter to be right in this regard. He who is right by the force of conscience is never so happy as he who is right by the force of love; for conscience is a hard master, and carries a straight rule. The more acute your conscience is to inspire you to duty, the more it torments you when you violate your duty. Conscience is a despot. It almost never smiles; it sits and scowls; and its business is to flagellate rather than reward: but love suffereth long, and is kind; love envieth not; love vaunteth not itself, is not puffed up, doth not behave itself unseemly, seeketh not her own, is not easily provoked, thinketh no evil. Love, transcendent, shall abide when doctrines, and ordinances, and churches, and governments shall have passed away—when nothing else shall remain but the other supeme moral sentiments of the soul—faith and hope. Love, even in that hour, high above either of these, and above all other things, high above them as the spire of a cathedral is above the roof or the foundations—shall exist; for it is God; and is yet to be God over all, blessed—because blessing—for ever and forever.

PRAYER BEFORE THE SERMON.

WE rejoice, our Father, that thou art leading our thoughts up to thee by all the associations of this sacred day; by the familiarities of friendship; by the rejoicing of love; by all the blessed memories which come to us in the calm and quiet of the Sabbath. We thank thee that the whole week doth not need to rush on with care and burden; and that we have a right to pause, and upon one whole day to rest in body and in soul, and to give our spirits, oppressed with labor and care, repose, or to give them incitement or instruction in the things that pertain to righteousness.

Wilt thou grant thy blessing to rest upon this day, and upon all that are present in this assembly, coming from a hundred experiences, bearing each his own thread of history, with sorrows not alike but in common, with joys also in common, and yet strangely different. O Lord, as thou dost look upon every heart here, and see that it is in weakness and sinfulness, and in everlasting need of God's help, grant that to every one may be given, this morning, that quickening Spirit which bears to the soul peace, and purity, and the sense of forgiveness and inspiration, so that courage, and hope, and joy may spring up from associations with thee. We need thy help, and thou art most helpful. We need thy forgiveness, and thou art most long-suffering, forgiving iniquity, transgression and sin. Thou art patient with those who are seeking, even in the least degree, to live aright; and assistance cometh to them from the divine offices of the Spirit. Not the sun, traveling in the greatness of his strength, sheds more light and life than thou, in the greater strength of thy nature, O Sun of righteousness, that dost come with healing in thy beams. Vouchsafe to every one in thy presence, this morning, we pray thee, the sanctifying influence of thy Spirit. We pray that thou wilt bless each one who puts forth the faintest endeavor to live better. May whatever is good in us ripen. May whatever is evil in us be more and more overruled. May we not refuse to go forward by sitting down in sinfulness and remorse, and forever looking backward and bemoaning our mistakes, or our want of improvement of privileges, or our sorrows in bereavement. May we forget what is behind. We are children not of the past, but of the future. We live by faith, and are filled with hope. May we look forward away from the mistakes and errors of the past. In the light of the hope that is in Christ Jesus, may we look forward and press forward toward the mark, for the prize of the high calling of God in Christ Jesus.

If there be those that are seeking to break down evil habits, give thou them, we beseech of thee, strength not only, but patience to persevere therein.

Be with those who are by every means endeavoring to build themselves up better, and more and more Christlike. Give them power to gain perfect dominion, at length, over every appetite, over every lust, over all selfishness, over pride, and envy, and jealousy, and every malign passion that is in the soul. And may all those that are seeking good help each other. Grant that there may be more pitifulness in our souls toward any whose purposes are good, but who are wafted hither and thither, not by their own will, but by that which is around about them.

We pray that we may be bound in sympathy even to those who are evil. May our hearts yearn for them as thy heart yearns for us. What should we have been but for the thought of God resting upon us, and for thy grace and patience with us? We should have been even as the poorest and most needy are. Let us, then, not be forgiven, and be the recipients every day of thy bounty, and consume it selfishly upon ourselves, turning censoriously upon those that are less favored than we, and condemn them, or pass them by with indifference. May we be joined in heart to those who are beneath and far away from us, even as we are joined in a blessed unity to thee and to thy Spirit.

Grant thy blessing to rest, we pray thee, to-day, upon this house, and all that dwell in it—upon those that direct and control it, and upon those that are recipients of their kindness. May thy blessing rest, also, upon all those who have gathered together here from neighboring places. Speak peace to every heart. Comfort the sorrowing. Strengthen the wavering. Inspire those who are discouraged. Give courage to men who are in places of peril, that they may resolutely, and with divine help, overcome their adversaries.

We pray that thou wilt follow our thoughts; for what Sabbath morning dawns upon the earth that our hearts do not search out whom we love everywhere? Some are in distant lands, some are upon the sea, some are in far remote places in our own land, and some sit sorrowful in their homes, waiting and watching. Wherever they are whom we love, love thou them this day, and bear to them some sense of our sympathy; and may our prayers fall as dews on flowers upon their heads.

Let thy blessing rest upon all the interests of this great land. Bless the President of these United States, and all those who are joined to him in authority. Bless the Governors of the different States, and the magistrates therein, and the citizens belonging thereto. Spread abroad the light of knowledge, we pray thee. May schools and seminaries of every kind flourish. May intelligence prevail throughout the whole land. And grant that this great nation may grow up in strength both outward and inward, not to tread down the poor, the weak, and the oppressed. May this nation not be filled with greed and avarice, but may it at last begin to shine abroad with the true light of Christian kindness, and become the defender of the helpless, and an example to those who are toiling in oppression. At last may that light come forth which shall emancipate the world. May men, touched with the divine Spirit, live again in their higher nature, and become too strong for manacles to hold them, and too wise for despots to oppress them. Thus may this whole world come to its liberty by coming to the Lord Jesus Christ, and receiving the new manhood that is in Christ Jesus.

And to thy name shall be the praise, Father, Son, and Spirit, evermore. *Amen.*

PRAYER AFTER THE SERMON.

LORD, grant thy blessing to rest upon us, to give us an understanding heart, not only, but to give us an applying disposition. Grant that the truth which we have heard may be as seed sown in good ground, springing up, and bringing forth a hundred fold. Pity those things which we blame in ourselves, and those things which we reprehend in others as their teachers. Have compassion upon us because we are sinners. Have compassion upon our motives. Have compassion upon all those faults which are full of weakness and selfishness. Thou that makest thy sun to rise on the good and bad alike, help us, because we need help. Thy goodness and our want join in one plea. Be merciful to us, and teach us to be merciful to each other. Spread abroad that large-mindedness and catholicity of feeling which shall unite us, with growing force, to thee and to our fellow-men, that at last we may understand thy law, that goes everywhere, disseminating liberty, being imperious, and yet full of freedom. May each one of us hear and obey the command, Thou shalt love the Lord thy God with all thy heart and thy neighbor as thyself. And to thy name shall be the praise, Father, Son, and Spirit, evermore. *Amen.*

III.

Luminous Hours.

LUMINOUS HOURS.

I purpose giving, this morning, mainly a historic discourse, tracing the line of events that preceded and immediately followed that scene of unparalleled simplicity and beauty of which we read in the opening service—the Transfiguration. I know of scarcely another point in the narrative of our Master's life, around which there are so many interesting questions, and from which may be drawn so many threads woven into instruction so perfectly, and of such importance.

The first question that arises is in regard to the time. As you will perhaps bear in mind, in the narrative that we read from Luke (for this event is described by Matthew in the 17th chapter, and by Mark in the 9th chapter, as well as by Luke in the 9th chapter) it is said, "About an eight days after, (that, evidently, is a phrase used as we say 'About a week,' or 'About ten days.' Both of the other evangelists say, 'After six days,') he took Peter and James and John, and went up into the mountain to pray." These three disciples seem to have been the most intelligent and the most useful of the disciple band. They were the ones that almost always accompanied the Saviour. They seem to have been men of some mark and character. Certainly they proved afterwards that they were more active than any of the others. James and John, the sons of Zebedee, were called "Sons of Thunder." They were men of work. And when the Saviour went off on any mission, he took Peter, James and John with him. You will recollect that the mother of John and James

Preached at the TWIN MOUNTAIN HOUSE, White Mountains, N. H., Sunday morning, Sept. 6th, 1874. Lesson: Luke ix., 28–42. Hymns (Plymouth Collection)· Nos 119 564, Doxology.

undertook to make them Prime Minister and Treasurer of the new kingdom, saying to Christ, "Grant that these my two sons may sit, the one on thy right hand, and the other on the left, in thy kingdom." They had a natural ascendency over the other disciples, and it excited envy and jealousy among them. The dispute on the way to Jerusalem, as to who of them should be greatest, came in part from this.

Now, Jesus took these three disciples, it is said, six days after. Six days after what? Well, so far as we have any information, after nothing. It reveals, in one sense, we may say, the loose way in which the gospels were constructed. What is the origin of the four lives of Christ? If Prescott should sit down to write the life of Ferdinand and Isabella he would first collect facts, dates, etc., belonging to their career, as guides or milestones by which he would travel through their history. These he would arrange, introducing the various characters, and unfolding their experiences, step by step, year by year, and putting them in the relation of cause and effect, of precedent and consequent.

Were the four Gospels written in that way? Did Matthew, under the divine inspiration, sit down, begin at the beginning, and go right straight through to the end? He did not. Neither did Mark, nor did Luke, who was the most methodical of all of the evangelists; nor did John, who wrote the last Gospel many, many years after the others were written.

It is to be remembered that our Master, so far as we know, never wrote a line. It is one of the things to be remarked with wonder, that that man, whose influence has been revolutionary in time, and on the globe, never put pen to paper. Not only that, but nothing went down as coming accurately from his lips, and by his direct authority—not one single scrap. All that we have of his sayings and teachings was caught up, as it were. The disciples were with him in the valleys, on the mountain sides, in obscure fishing villages, and in the despised province of Galilee; for at the crucifixion, you will recollect, it was said to them, "Your speech bewrays [betrays] you," and they were taunted as having come from Galilee. The inhabitants of Galilee were despised in Jerusalem as in Boston men are if they do not live in the "polished city;" as they are in New York, if they do not live in the "metropolitan city;" as they are in London, if they are not Londoners; and as they are in Paris, if they are not Parisians. These were refined men, and esthetic people, and orthodox folks, who regarded Galilee as a contemptible province. As the Jews despised the Gentiles, so the Greeks and Romans despised the provinces. And five-sixths, nine-tenths, nineteen-twentieths, of our Lord's life, was passed in that province. But his instructions there were not registered. He took no pains to have them sent out. He spoke them, and let them alone, and they rested simply in the memory of those who were around about him; and not a hundredth nor a thousandth part of them have been gathered up at all. The words of John are very significant where, using an oriental extravagance and employing metaphorical language, he says, "There are also many things which Jesus did, the which, if they should be written every one, I suppose that even the world itself could not contain the books that should be written."

It always seemed strange to me, since there was such immense fruitfulness of discourse in our Master, that there never came to us anything except that which is embalmed in the four Gospels. One would think that the intelligent philosophers of his day might have caught something, and the heathen something, and thus at least single sentences would have been handed down to us; but I have looked through all the pseudo and counterfeit gospels of the third and fourth centuries, and in other works outside of the New Testament, and I have found nothing that looks like a possible sentence uttered by our Lord, save one. It seems as though this might have been spoken by him. It is recorded in an old book that he was walking along the road and saw a man working on Sunday, or on the Sabbath, as they would call it, and said, "If thou understandest what thou art doing, blessed art thou; but if thou understandest it not, thou art accursed." That is to say, "If thou hast so large an idea of a man's life as to look upon the Sabbath day as his servant, and not his master, and thou art working in that broad sphere of intelligence, blessed art thou, because thou art emancipated; but if thou believest the Sabbath day to be a day of bondage and a law over all, and in defiance of that art working on it, accursed art thou." This sounds very much like the Master. It resembles many sayings of his. Besides that, I know not of a single other one that is to be found out of the Holy Scriptures.

How, then, came the Gospels into being? What is the origin of them? Well, those who heard him went out and repeated what they heard. Of course there would be hundreds of men talking up and down in the villages, and telling what they heard him say, and what they saw him do. By and by one would distort the truth a little, and another would distort it a little more; and after some twenty years it became apparent that there were so many different versions as to make it necessary that somebody should give authentic statements. So Matthew, who companied with Christ, wrote the first Gospel; Luke wrote another; Mark, another; and St. John the last. It is said that St. John wrote his at the request of the elders of Ephesus, in order to include in it some teachings that Christ gave, of which the other Gospels had nothing.

On what principle did they construct the Gospels? Suppose in a village where there are a dozen officers, intelligent men, who went with Sherman on his march to the sea, they should come together and talk about that campaign. One would tell a story; that would suggest another which somebody else would tell, and that would suggest another. One man would say what he saw, another what he saw, and another what he saw. So it would go round and round the circle; and the whole evening would be spent in that way. The principle on which they would relate their separate narratives would be association. They would not attempt to give a connected history. One man's story would make another man think of something that happened five years before; and that would make another man think of something that happened two years after. The different narratives would be thrown together, so far as the time element is concerned, in confusion; and yet every particle would be true.

Now, the evangelists put their accounts together in very much the same manner. The Gospels are not constructed in any order of time or dates. The facts which are recorded in them stand in the order of suggestion and association. One is given, and another, and another; and when you come to connect dates with them, you find, perhaps, that a thing which happened near the close of the Saviour's life is placed at the beginning, and that a thing which took place near the beginning of his life is placed toward the close. It is evident from the mixed way in which the events stand that there was a very loose manner of combining them. This is shown in the very first clause of the passage which we read—"About eight days after." After what, is not stated. The writer had something in his mind which he did not record.

We have, then, to look into the evangelists more closely to see where it was and when it was that the steps were begun which led to this grand culmination on the mountain top, —this transcendent vision of glory—and what those steps were. Our Saviour's whole active ministry probably did not overrun fifteen months. The great bulk of his miracles and instruction were included in one year. It has generally been said that there were three years of his ministry; but the active part of those three years did not reach much over one year, and according to the best modern scholars did not extend beyond fifteen months; and of this time perhaps all but two months—one spent actively in Judæa and one in Peræa— was spent in Galilee.

It was in Galilee that his fame began. What was the reason of that fame? The reason of it, when you come to trace it back to the very root, was that he was the most perfect Jew that the Jews had ever seen or heard. It is very striking to see, in looking through the life of Christ, the sentiment of patriotism that he touched. He was a Jew after the strictest type. He knew that he was descended from the old and revered ancestral Jewish stock. He conformed to the usages of the Jews. He observed the Sabbath day. He worshiped in the synagogue. He went to Jerusalem to attend the great feasts. He represented, to the common people, in whose hearts the sentiment of patriotism was the strongest, the perfect Jew. When he began to work miracles, they said, "Another prophet has come." The instruction that followed his guileless life; his wonder-workings; his appeals, not so much to the reason as to the moral sentiments; his kindness and familiarity; his going about and doing good, in contrast with the haughtiness of the Pharisees, and with the selfishness that belonged to the dominant party at that time in the Jewish economy; his sympathy for the poor, the sick, the necessitous of every name—these things won the great multitude to him, and they regarded him as a prophet in that long line of Jewish prophets of whom they were proud, and of whom the whole world has become justly proud, because among them have been some of the grandest moral natures that ever lived. There have been men in history that illumined philosophy, and developed power, and achieved military glory; but nowhere has the moral element been more conspicuous than in the Jewish nation, of which men nowadays are sometimes so much ashamed. The faith of our fathers, their conscience, and their hope of immortality, all sprang from that wonderful people; and Jesus seemed to his own countrymen to be the most illustrious among them. They felt that their time had come. This proud nation, on which the Roman yoke lay, and which the Assyrian had trampled into the dust, but which inherited the promises of God, longed for emancipation; they looked and waited for it. And, at last, there came among them a man, spotless, wise, and of wonderful power with God and with men, and he carried the hearts of the common people with him, as being the best Jew that ever lived in their modern times. When miracle after miracle was wrought by him, the Pharisees found fault; but the common people were on his side; and all the time they had this latent feeling: "He will very soon disclose himself; the old banner will outroll again, he will draw his sword, the promises shall be fulfilled, and no longer shall we be the tail but we shall be the head; all nations shall come and worship at Jerusalem, and we shall be God's right favored trusty stock; we shall convert the Gentiles, and then the whole earth shall be redeemed." So they watched him with great expectation;

and days and weeks went by, and the blind received their sight, and the lame walked, the lepers were cleansed, the deaf heard, the dead were raised, and the poor had the gospel preached to them; and they said, "When will the time come—everything is on the way to it, but when will it come—that he will declare himself the Messiah?"

It was to the north-east shore of the sea of Tiberias, or Galilee, that Christ went, not long before the occurrence of this scene, to rest. Overborne with the fatigue of instruction, he told his disciples to get with him into a ship, or boat, and they went thither with him. When the multitudes heard that he had gone there they ran around the lake shore, out of their cities and villages, to join him. The average distance was not above six miles. It was not further than that, even from Capernaum. At one point the mountain came down to the very sea. Between that and the mouth of the Jordan there was a large plain. There it was that the Saviour landed; and it is said that there were some five thousand persons there, besides the women and children; so that there could not have been much less than ten thousand people gathered there. He rested and taught them all day; and when evening came his heart was filled with compassion toward them on account of their hunger—for the Saviour thought of bread-and-butter as well as of catechism. He thought of men's bodies as well as of their souls. He had regard for physical as well as for spiritual wants. There were ten thousand people without food assembled before him at that time, and then it was that he performed the miracle of feeding the multitude. That was the most undisguised miracle of the whole series. There was no deception about it. If you think that a man can carry food for ten thousand persons in his pockets, or that he can conceal it in the caves of a mountain and surprise them with it, you are greatly mistaken. There could have been no such thing as collusion in this case. Imagine how much it would take to feed ten thousand people, so that there should be enough, and twelve baskets over. He took the five loaves and the two fishes, and multiplied them, and multiplied them, until the ten thousand persons, men, women and children, were fed, under circumstances that made it evident that it must be a divine power that was at work. There was no getting around it. If he had raised a man from the dead they might have said, "Oh, he had just fainted away;" if he had restored some person that was sick of a fever, they might have said, "Well, there are doctors that can heal the sick by magnetic influence;" but no man can feed ten thousand folks from five loaves and two fishes by anything short of superhuman power. It was one of the most convincing of miracles; the people were convinced; and they said, "Indeed, unquestionably, this is our long-promised Leader." It is recorded that then they undertook to take him by force and make him king. That was the point of the highest popular enthusiasm. Then it was that the wave broke and overwhelmed them with disappointment, for he not only refused to be king, but he determined to depart. The disciples themselves were caught up in the popular enthusiasm, and that single sentence is very significant where it is said, "He constrained [compelled] the disciples to get into a ship, and to go before him unto the other side." They were so wrought up with the multitude that he was obliged to exercise his authority over them, and take hold of Peter, and say, "Get into that boat," and to push John in, and send them off. Having sent them off, he went back to the mountain to pray.

What was there in that refusal to be king that should damage him? Any man who is curious of human nature, and watches to see how the heart and mind work, knows how, in our day, where there is a cause in which men are engaged, as for instance the temperance cause, they become enthusiastic, and their leaders eagerly zealous. Let a minister in a parish, during a temperance excitement, preach that to abstain from intoxicating drinks is well, to be sure, but that he does not want to sign the pledge; let him say, "I believe that every man should be temperate, but I do not think it necessary for him to bind himself never to touch a drop of liquor," and the foremost reformers will say, "He goes to the edge, but he won't go in body and soul and help carry on this work;" and they dislike him more than they do drinkers, and oftentimes more than they do liquor dealers themselves. Men who are conducting a reform want people to come in or keep out; they do not want any half-way folks connected with them.

Now, the Jews were full of expectancy; they thought the time was coming nearer and nearer when he was to declare himself as their king; their hearts grew warmer and warmer, and their enthusiasm burned higher and higher until the climax was reached,—and then he turned away and utterly refused to be king; and when the disciples attempted to persuade him he warned them off, and sent them back into the boat, and departed himself to the mountain. The people were disappointed in him, and said, "He is a sham; he is a pretender; he has no heart, no nerve, no bone and muscle; he is nothing;" and that was the end of his popularity.

You will recollect how, that same night, when the disciples were on the sea, he came to them walking on the water, and quieting the wind which was "contrary unto them." And they came ashore and landed at Magdala, a little south of Capernaum, on the northwest coast of Galilee. There he was met, we are told, by the Pharisees, by the Scribes, and by the Herodians. The Pharisees represented the most orthodox people among the Jews. The Scribes were their teachers, their doctors, their lawyers, the most learned and eminent men that they had among them. The Sadducees represented the philosophic element. They were not very religious, but they made up in ambition what they lacked in other respects. At this time the Sadducees were in great power; I think both the high-priests were Sadducees. The Herodians represented political ideas and influences of the reigning court. So at Magdala Christ met the orthodoxy of the Jews, the scholarship of the Jews, the advanced philosophy of the Jews, and the regnant politics of the nation. Every element of power among the people he found waiting for him. And when he undertook to teach them, their ears were shut to him on every side. Unfaith and scornfulness confronted him whichever way he turned. He found himself rejected everywhere. And he was not spared from ridicule. When he spoke of the bread from heaven, men said to him, "Why don't you give us that bread?"

Contempt was heaped upon him in every form. He was met with the most caustic, bitter, taunting feelings.

At this place Christ took a ship, with his disciples, and sailed up the coast to Bethsaida Julius. He also went to Chorazin. Capernaum was likewise visited by him. There he was grieved and heart-sick, as he was leaving Galilee for the last time. Then it was that he looked wistfully at the cities on the hill, where he had spent so much time, and said,

"Woe unto thee, Chorazin! woe unto thee, Bethsaida! for if the mighty works which were done in you had been done in Tyre and Sidon, they would have repented long ago in sackcloth and ashes. But I say unto you, it shall be more tolerable for Tyre and Sidon at the day of judgment than for you. And thou, Capernaum, which art exalted into heaven shalt be brought down to hell; for if the mighty works which have been done in thee had been done in Sodom, it would have remained until this day."

Landing at Bethsaida Julius, he heals a blind man, and then goes on far north to get out of the way of the rabble, and to escape insult. To tell the truth, Jesus was tired; he was worn out—for he had a body, and it behooved him to be like his brethren; his spirits were sucked up; and he longed for solitude. So he went to the very bounds of Palestine, northward to Cesaræa Philippi, called "the coast [*i. e.* the borders] of Tyre and Sidon." It was in the neighborhood of these cities; but he did not go to them, so far as we know. He attempted to hide himself; and he gave injunctions that nobody should be told where he was.

Here opened the history of the Syrophœnician woman, who brought to him her daughter that was possessed; and it was in close connection with this that the Transfiguration took place.

This leads me to say that in the account of his ascending the high mountain at evening, no mention is made of the place—a circumstance which brings to mind again the singular manner in which the Gospels were constructed. Mount Tabor, which is to the southwest of Capernaum in Galilee, has been said to be the mount of Transfiguration; but it is morally certain that it was not, for the reason that from immemorial it was a hill fortified by a citadel. Josephus speaks of strengthening its works, so that it must have been a place frequented by soldiers and peoble. It is impossible that Mount Tabor should have been the scene of the Transfiguration. History rather points out that this scene occurred on the skirt, or one of the bounds of Mount Hermon—a snow-clad mountain that never lifted the white cap from its head. There it was that Jesus went at night with Peter, James and John.

It was a custom of Orientals, as it is now, after wrapping their head with a mantle and saying their prayers, to instantly lie down and fall asleep, (men in the open air sleep easily.) At evening our Saviour ascended high up on the flanks of Hermon, and these three men were asleep, as they were in the garden afterwards; and Jesus now, as then, prayed; and while he prayed a great change came over his appearance. It is said that his face did shine as the sun; and his raiment was white and glistering—exceeding white, like the snow. It is not said that he was lifted up, though Raphael, in his picture of the Transfiguration, makes him so; but that he stood wonderfully changed in his whole aspect is the sum of the declaration of the Gospels.

There appeared also Moses and Elias. Why they? Why not angels? Why not, as at Christ's temptation, and at his baptism, personages of celestial origin? You are to remember that the old dispensation was about to cease in power for the sake of giving place to the new—that is to say, as the blossom falls in order that the fruit may swell under it, and be better than the blossom, so the old dispensation was the blessed flower of ages from which has come the noblest fruit that the world ever saw; it was fit that there should be witnesses from the old dispensation; and there were not two names belonging to that dispensation which were more illustrious than those of Moses and Elias, or Elijah—the Hebrew name is stronger than the Greek. Moses was the grandest law-giver, and Elijah was the noblest prophet and reformer, of his time. They stood magnificent as the pyramids of Egypt. Abraham, Isaac and Jacob were treasured names; but these men never did or said much that was worth remembering. No philosophy, no organization, no new order in the state, and no development of spirit-life, ever sprung from them. They were simply magnificent pictorial heads and fountains of Jewish stock. They were pious, pure, and mildly sagacious. Their nation was proud of them as of mythical men. When it came to the matter of national growth and reform they were of no account. Moses was the greatest man of antiquity; and I think I may say that even in modern times a greater than he has never walked the earth. Wondrous was his career beyond the power of words to paint. At forty he began and was cast out; then he spent forty years more in the wilderness as in a school of solitude; and then at eighty, when most men are ready to lay down the burden of life, he took it up and commenced the work of emancipating and organizing the men of the wilderness. At the age of a hundred and twenty years his eye was not dimmed, and he left a record which has not died out. There never has been a commonwealth, and there never will be one, without having the marrow and bone and muscle of Moses put into it. Absolutely, his was one of the greatest names of the world, and it was unquestionably the greatest name of antiquity.

The name of Elijah was also illustrious. When the kingdom seemed about to be destroyed, when Ahab the idolatrous, and Jezebel the infamous, caused the prophets of God to be hunted, then came this man as a flame of lightning and a burst of thunder from the wilderness, and undaunted he put down the king, and slew the prophets of Baal, and restored the kingdom, and exerted such an influence that his name to this hour is talismanic in the history of the Jews; so that when they have their Pentecostal feast, or Passover, there is always a chair left for Elijah, as with an expectation of his coming.

These two men stood transfigured as the angels of heaven, and Christ was transfigured between them. What was the theme of their conversation in this august drama? His death, that he should accomplish at Jerusalem.

When you consider the solitude of the mountain, the cool air, and the green grass upon which they were, and the magnificent background of glacier-capped Hermon; when you consider that it was night, and that the three disciples lay sleeping while this magnificent picture was passing before them, — a transcendent Gospel before men dead, as it were —when you consider these things, you must feel that this was one of the most illustrious spots of the whole history of the New Testament.

Just as these figures were disappearing, Peter, James, and John awoke; and they saw the brightness and the glory as they were fainting, fainting, fainting and going out in the air; and Peter, the impetuous, who always spoke first and afterwards thought what he had said, exclaimed, "O Master! let us stay here forever. Let us build three tabernacles—one for thee, and one for Moses, and one for Elias;"—"for he wist not what he said," as it is recorded; and he is not the only descendant of the apostles who has not known what he was talking about, when speaking on such subjects! The Master adjured them that they should tell no man.

Then of these figures that were luminous, the two departed. Christ apparently resumed his natural aspect; but the whole heaven was as one great beaming mass of light; and a vision shone upon them; and out of that cloud as from a voice of thunder came the words, "My beloved Son—hear ye him;" and then the vision departed.

This doubtless took place between midnight and the dawn. When the morning had come, Jesus took his disciples and began to talk to them about his approaching trial and death. They descended with him from the mountain; and when they had reached the base the people saw him coming, and were surprised and amazed. It seems that he retained something of the appearance which he had on the mountain top, and they ran to him. Soon he found his disciples in an altercation with the Pharisees. Then occurred a scene which was the antithesis of that of the Syrophœnician woman. A father met Jesus at the bottom of the mountain, and no dramatic literature has anything to be compared with that father's petition for his son. Christ healed the son, and then he passed on, and went south again.

Thus far for the external history. Now the question arises, in the first place, What was the intent of the Transfiguration? Why was such a passage of history as this developed in the economy of the New Testament?

It is a matter profoundly to be grateful for, that our Saviour was bodily tired at times; that he was hungry at times; that he was an outcast at times; that he had not where to lay his head; that he was homesick. Said he, "The foxes have holes, the birds of the air have nests, but I have not where to lay my head." There is nothing in literature more touching than the homesickness of Christ. He had wrought in his miraculous way and in his teaching way, until his spirit and body seemed spent; he had come to the very climax of popularity; he had been rejected by the common people; and going back to the west side of the lake he was disowned by the men of his own nation. He was a Jew, and he had the spirit of patriotism which belonged to the Jew; and no man who loves his nation can bear to be set aside from it.

I know that in the old days of the Anti-slavery conflict there was nothing that ever pierced my soul more bitterly than the thought that I loved this whole land, and was shut out from more than half of it. I knew that my heart's desire was to have the whole nation prosperous, illustrious, grand; and to know that that longing was met with scorn and contempt hurt me. I thought I understood how Christ felt when he was rejected by his own people.

So, spent by labor and worn out by grief of heart, he yearned for the wilderness. No man attempts to do great things for his time and for his people, that he does not long for the wilderness. The more you love men, the more, sometimes, it is impossible to endure them; at times you go into the forest, when trees seem more to you than men with their selfishness, uncharitableness, and hardness; and it is a comfort to me to know that my Master was homesick and worksick, and longed to get into the wilderness, where no man could find him.

He needed more than that. Christ being under human conditions, and suffering what humanity suffers, was discouraged; and it was necessary that he should be built up again. Therefore he ascended into the divine communion; and it pleased God, by the opening of the heavens, and by those messengers of the old dispensation that were adapted to pour balm and consolation into his heart who was working for the new, to give him re-invigoration.

O man of God, preaching in the wilderness, tired, disheartened, and accusing yourself of a want of courage and faith, your Master was tired, and needed angelic ministration to set him up for his work.

O woman in some despoiled neighborhood, bearing the burden of the household, and longing to do something for the school, or for the needy of the neighborhood, unhelped, alone and discouraged, and often wishing yourself dead, you tread in the footsteps of Him who once walked the earth, but who now reigns in heaven.

O ye that are seeking the world's gain, either in your family or in the community; ye that embrace in your thought and ambition the ages and nations, do not be ashamed that you experience hours of deep depression; for Christ had them, and he sanctified them to the good of men. Like him, too, you may have times of luminousness and emancipation. On the mountain-top, unexpectedly, in the night, when all is darkness, there may come to you the radiancy of a revelation from the heavenly land.

Jesus Christ was walking with his face toward Jerusalem, his heavens were filled with thunder-bolts, stroke on stroke fell upon him, he was subjected to torment and suffering, and he needed, by influences from above, to be armed for the next and last scene—that of his forty days' passion.

More than that, did he not foresee that the events then taking place were more than likely to scatter his disciples, to frighten and dishearten them, so that he would be quite forsaken by them? He did.

The Transfiguration was meant primarily for his comfort. Next, it was meant for the comfort of the apostles. Peter, James and John were to go with him to Jerusalem. There he was to have a season of conflict with the scholars before he went to the peasantry. He was to go among the educated Jews, to be put into the hands of wicked men, to be crucified, and to be buried out of sight.

You recollect the beautiful narrative given in Luke, of the walk to Emmaüs. You remember how bewildered they were; how Christ walked with them unknown to them. You have not forgotten how he held their eyes so that they could not tell who he was. When they said they had hoped that Jesus was he who was to be the deliverer, but that he was destroyed, then Christ opened his mouth and taught them out of the Scriptures, and showed them how it was necessary that the Saviour should be put to death, and rise again. That was a very perilous period for the disciples, during which their Master was cut off and entombed, and when there was nothing for their senses—for their sensuous mind—for their bodily sight, and they had not yet learned faith; what was it that under such circumstances held the disciple band together?

Do you know that the imagination is a stronger element than the reason? You might suspect it by the fact that the Bible employs imagination ten times where it does philosophy once.

When old people go back to their childhood, what things do they remember most? Arguments? Not at all. What do you remember about your mother that is gone? Not anything by which she was formally made known to the world, but some picture, some scene of tenderness, some fragrant sentiment which lingers in your imagination.

What is it of your friends that you remember longest? Not the shape of their eye-brows, or of their face, which was drawn as they sat like a wooden dunce having their portrait made, but that expression which they had when they came to the door and looked in and glanced at you; or which flashed over their face when at table some story was told. You remember that. You never will forget it. The memory of man is kept alive by dreams, by superstitions, or by pictures which appeal to the imagination and the fancy. These things get a hold upon you which can never be lost.

Now, when the disciples went down to Jerusalem, and they saw Christ indefensible, arrested, carried before tribunals, subjected to a mock trial, condemned, dragged forth ignominiously, taunted, lifted upon the cross, in darkness and anguish, dying; when they saw his enemies triumphant and exultant, and saw Christ buried, and saw the stone rolled up and the tomb sealed, and saw guards placed to watch the sepulcher, there was every inducement in the world for them to have said to themselves, "We have been living like a bubble, and it has burst,—it is ended and gone"; and they could not give a reason for thinking it was not gone. There was nothing that they could put their hands upon which helped their faith; but they remembered how Christ looked when working miracles, when performing deeds of mercy, and when standing before them in transfiguration on the top of the mountain with the old prophets, and talking with them, when the cloud overshadowed them, from which the voice addressed them. This wonderful mountain-top picture they remembered. Against their reason and their senses there was something in their hearts that said, "We cannot give it up"; and they held on till the stone flew back and Christ appeared again to their longing, loving vision.

As, then, the Transfiguration was to comfort the heart of Jesus, so it was to prepare the disciples for the tribulation which was before them, and to hold them steadfast unto the end.

Christian brethren, there is some instruction to you and to me which ought to be drawn out of this beautiful picture. To me it has been as a bosom to a child. I have sucked at it as a babe at its mother's breast, and have been made stronger, healthier, patienter, better, by that which flows to me from this heavenly vision of the Transfiguration.

In the first place, to every one of us, first or last, come these luminous hours. I do not believe but that everybody has an opening heaven and thoughts that lift him above the vulgar present. I believe that everybody has heroic hours, generous hours, hours in which the superiority of the true, the good, the beautiful, is not any mere speculation, but a sensation, I might almost say a conviction. Everybody, I think, has his radiant hours of inspiration. But, alas! most men use these hours simply as hours of courtesy, or hours of luxury, and they say, "Oh, if we could always feel so! Oh, if we could always be just as we were at the end of that meeting, when the last hymn was sung, and the last stanza was rounded out gloriously! Oh, if we could always be as we were at the winding up of such a sermon, that taught and inspired us! Oh, if we could always live in such moods as we come into sometimes, alone, in meditation or prayer!"

But they are transient. Men do not see them perhaps for months, and sometimes not for years. They are not concatenated. They do not become our life at all. And transfiguration seven times a week, I think, would become uninstructive. It is solitariness that makes a thing striking. Things that we do over and over again every day are trite and make no impression upon us. Those hours of illumination which God gives to men are precious hours; and you want to repeat them. You want to build tabernacles and sit down in them. Some men's idea of being a Christian is to have a good time; to sing hymns till they feel like angels. They want to be on the mountain-top, out of the reach of turmoil, while at the bottom of the mountain the devil is at work destroying men. They do not want to be in the midst of sorrow and suffering, where they will see tears and hear groans. They want to enjoy themselves, and let the world go. Peter prayed for that; but it was not his business, and it is not yours, nor is it mine. Thank God for the hours of brightness which come to us, and thank God for the hours that must come to us, one after another, of burdens and troubles. Being a Christian does not take you out of life, nor redeem you from the laws of this world, or from social disturbances, or from political exigencies. We are workers together with God, where tears fall, where breaking hearts are, and where sorrows gush like springs from mountains. Here is where we live, and where we should be; and if we are occasionally taken into those higher experiences, let us bless God for them, and use them to strengthen ourselves for lower ones. Many and many a man is working out his salvation better in tears and under burdens than when he seems to himself an angel about to fly to the kingdom of glory. It is not when you feel best that you are best, but when you suffer most and most patiently under trials and misfortunes. Not when God is lifting men up, but when he is pressing them down, is he blessing them most.

Not when he rides into the city after a victory is the general most noble, but when he is in the wilderness, and everything is dark and lowering, and by his courage and indomitable perseverance he overcomes obstacles. It is when a man rises above his circumstances and moods that true manhood shows itself in him. It is then that he is grandest and nearest to God.

There is another thing. As the Transfiguration on the mount was designed to teach the disciples how to conduct themselves when the exigencies which were to come upon them should be developed, so these luminous hours which come to all men ought to be used by them to determine their duties and courses. "What shall a man do?" is a question that is occurring every single day; and what a man shall do will be settled by a higher or lower court. The lower court of man's nature, where pride and selfishness and avarice and vanity reside, almost always settles questions, and it almost always settles them wrong. What is generous? Is it best to act generously? What is liberal? How much ought a man to be liberal? What is self-sacrifice? How far ought a man in justice to himself and his family to be self-sacrificing?— these questions are generally settled by the lower court of the human mind. It says, "Take care of yourself: if every man would take care of one, the whole world would be taken care of." A man's first impulse, if he be a man, is to do the best, the noblest, the ripest thing; but he says, "Let me take a second thought"; and that second thought always lowers the tone of his manliness.

A man says, "I thought I would give fifty dollars; but I think I will give only twenty-five." He thinks again, and says, "There are so many people here that I don't believe I need to give more than ten dollars." Before the box comes round he thinks again; and he does not give more than a dollar. In those hours when your best nature is in the ascendency; when the reason is calm and the moral feelings are alive; when you are impelled by motives from the side furthest away from the beast—then is the best time to settle questions of doubt and procedure. In your best hours take your highest thoughts, and follow them.

Some of you, in many hours, doubt whether there is any God. Some of you doubt whether there is any validity in the Bible. Some of you doubt whether there is any good except as circumstances favor. Those doubts and skepticisms every man, whose mind is active, and who is observing, has, more or less, in his lower hours; and they dampen and hinder him; but at other times he looks beyond the expanse of this life, and over the horizon, and he has a sense of the certainty and nearness of God; and his whole soul adjudicates. *Then* it is that he should take his reckoning, fix his landmarks and steer by them.

When a man goes over the Alleghanies, or any untrodden mountain, on some hill-top he looks forward and sees how the whole land lies; and he singles out some vast rock, some tall pine, or some prominent point, as a land mark; then he goes down into the champaign, and the way is no longer open like a map before him. He is lost; but still he keeps the general direction; and by and by, through a little opening, he sees yonder rock or pine or point; and he says, "Ah! that is what I saw," and travels on, and emerges again. Pretty soon he disappears again in the valley, but keeping the direction, he soon rises again so that his landmark comes into view once more.

It is when you are on the mountain-top that you should take your landmarks and steer toward them, and when you go down and lose sight of them, keep straight across the valley until you rise so that they greet your vision again. Not when you are in the valley can you tell which way to travel, unless you have learned it on the top of the hill.

One single other thing. After all the beauty and sublimity of this wonderful miracle wrought upon the person of Jesus Christ, and after all the instruction connected with it, it still comes back to me in the light of the apostle's joyful yet sad utterance, "Now we see through a glass, darkly; but then face to face." We are all of us ignorant; we know in part; we are partialists; nobody knows a great deal; but the time is drawing near, Christian brethren, when neither upon this mountain, nor at Jerusalem, nor upon Mount Hermon, nor upon any earth-summit, shall we need to receive instruction, or have any luminous hours, or pass through this or that experience; but when we shall stand in Zion and before God, and shall see him as he is, and shall be like him, and shall rejoice with him forever and forever.

May God so incline your hearts to wisdom, your souls to love, and your lives to faith and to a holy obedience, that when, brighter a thousand times than the Mount of Transfiguration, the vision of God shall rise upon you in the other life, your eye shall not blench, and your heart shall not be daunted.

He it is for whom I have waited. This is He for whom my soul has longed. I have traveled through time, and twilight, and midnight, and sorrow; but I behold Him, and it is enough. The blessing is begun, and it shall end never.

PRAYER BEFORE THE SERMON.

WE bless thee, our Father, for the clear light of truth, dawning in the early day, and gathering strength with the ages. It shines brighter and brighter unto the perfect day. Forgive us that we have so much light, and yet go stumbling along the way of life. Forgive us that we, standing under the influences of two worlds, are scarcely able to know and understand the laws of one, and obey them. We acknowledge our weakness; the sense of our sinfulness is always with us; but thou art gracious. Thou dwellest in love unspeakable. We build with selfishness and pride. We, creatures of the dust, and ruled by material influences, hardly yet understand, even in our choicest experiences, what are the greatness, and the wisdom, and the power and the discipline of divine love. We rejoice that thy government is established thereupon. We rejoice that God is love, and that yet he will control the universe so that all things shall work together for good, and that tears shall be wiped away, and groans shall cease, and sorrows shall roll their ceaseless waves no more for ever, and that there shall be no more hurting, and no more sickness, and no more crying, and no more death. How far away this land of vision is we know not; through how many ages yet the world must travail in pain we do not know; but it is a joy to our heart to believe that this radiant future is the consummation, and that toward it all things are steering. Whatever may be the mischances, whatever may be the interruptions and hindrances, however long the term may be, yet there shall come a day when all things shall be gathered up, and when to our Lord and Saviour Jesus Christ every knee shall bow, and every tongue confess, of things in heaven and things on earth, to the glory of God the Father. And we rejoice that when the end shall come, he will deliver up the authority, and God will be supreme, all in all. Our reason cannot follow. Our imagination staggers. What the radiant glory of that far-off development and perfectness of being shall be we cannot tell; but we hope, and fashion to ourselves in a thousand effervescent ways, and by a thousand pictures that come and go, the blessedness of that estate in which we shall dwell with God.

May the light of hope cheer us. May there fall down from heaven upon our souls, to-day, some brightness and joy that shall enable us to be stronger, more courageous and hopeful, and better able to endure unto the end.

Especially we beseech of thee, draw near to thy servants that are gathered together here this morning, and surprise those that have come not knowing why they came, and cheer those that have come hoping to meet thee. Lift the light of thy countenance upon those who dare not raise their eyes unto thee, being children of sorrow, bound fast and hopeless, if such there be.

Grant, O Lord, that thy light may come to those who sit in the valley and shadow of death. Make thyself again, as on earth thou didst declare thyself to be, the opener of prison-doors; the breaker of bands and shackles; the emancipator, leading forth those who are bound in dungeons. Give release to consciences that are bound and imprisoned. Give release to those who are endungeoned by doubts, and to those who are hopeless by reason of outward troubles. Break the yoke that is oppressive, and put upon the neck the yoke that is light and easy.

Grant, we beseech of thee, that Jesus Christ may be known to all who are here to-day, as the great presentation of God; as the helpful and suffering Father; as the one who bears the burdens of the universe, and carries all things in his arms toward universal victory. Grant that we may have rising upon our thoughts to-day a conception of the Healer, the Sun of Righteousness, that every one of us may be able to come under his wings, and be brooded of God.

We pray that thou wilt bless the little ones—the children that are growing up. May God guide them to honor, and fidelity, and true manliness and piety. We pray that their parents may both set a godly example before them, and know how to train them, as well as to teach them.

Bless, we pray thee, the families that are gathered together. Search out all their needs. Help every one of them to trust in God, and to bring that trust to bear on the affairs of life.

We beseech of thee that thou wilt go with our thoughts everywhere to-day as we remember those who are left behind, and those who have gone forth upon the great sea, and those who are scattered abroad throughout the continent. Will the Lord bless abundantly those who are absent from us. Thy heart is larger and warmer than ours. Take the measure of thy benefaction, not from our thinkings, but from thine own nature; and overflow the souls not only of those present, but of those absent ones who are dear to us.

We beseech of thee that thou wilt bless this neighborhood, and all the region around about. Bless all this great congregation in their gathering together this day to worship God. We beseech of thee that in the stillness and sweetness of this mountain retreat, the presence of that God who spoke from Mount Sinai and from Mount Calvary may be felt. May this be a Sabbath of calmness and peace in the souls of multitudes.

May a blessing accompany those who go hence. Grant that all the villages and neighborhoods may be visited by thy salvation.

Be pleased, O God, to remember our whole land, and all classes and conditions that are in it. Remember those who are spoiled and broken up in life, and are dying of despondency. Remember those who are outcast in ignorance, and know not how to conduct their lives well. We ask thy mercy for all those who are seeking knowledge, discouraged, in twilight, but who yet are looking toward the East for the dawning of intelligence.

Grant, we beseech of thee, thy blessing upon the States of this Union. May all those bonds that have been broken be reunited more firmly than ever. May all causes of offense, and dislike, and hatred be purged away, and may justice, and love, and reciprocal interests, and common patriotism, and longing for the welfare of the world around about us and lying in wickedness, be ushered in. Unite us inseparably that the nation may, following the example of the Lord

Jesus Christ, use its power, not for the despoiling of the poor and the weak, but rather for their building up on every hand.

Bless the President of these United States, and all who are joined with him in authority. Bless all the Governors of the several States of this nation, all judges and magistrates, and the great people. And grant that thy kingdom may come, and thy will be done, in this land as in heaven.

These mercies we ask through Jesus Christ our Redeemer. *Amen.*

PRAYER AFTER THE SERMON.

OUR Father, bless to us the truth which we have spoken. Bless to us the scenes that are recorded in thy holy word. Grant that we who interpret that word so poorly may discern more fruit and instruction in it than we have been wont to think it contained. May we learn more and more easily from it. Yet, may it not supersede the experiences of our lives, nor the revelations that thou art making to every person in his family, and in all his way and work. Bless thy word to those who are impatient of the disciplines and trials of thy providence, and to those whose hearts are set against the truth. Bless all thy servants in the varied lines of their duty. And bring us, with all whom thou lovest upon the earth—oh, bring us, ransomed and redeemed, into the kingdom of thy heavenly glory. And we will give the praise to the Father, the Son, and the Spirit, evermore. *Amen.*

IV.

LAW AND LIBERTY.

LAW AND LIBERTY.

" For, brethren, ye have been called unto liberty; only use not liberty for an occasion to the flesh, but by love serve one another. For all the law is fulfilled in one word, even in this: Thou shalt love thy neighbor as thyself. But if ye bite and devour one another, take heed that ye be not consumed one of another. This I say then, Walk in the Spirit, and ye shall not fulfill the lust of the flesh. For the flesh lusteth against the Spirit, and the Spirit against the flesh; and these are contrary the one to the other; so that ye cannot do the things that ye would. But if ye be led by the Spirit, ye are not under the law."—Gal. v., 13-18.

Of all the writers whose words are recorded in the Bible, there was no one whose spirit so perfectly accorded, on the whole, with the modern spirit, and the spirit which prevails in America, as Paul's. There was no one who had such a profound sense of individualism, of the right of the individual, or of the object of religion—namely, to build up in each particular person a manhood that should be large, strong, rich, and perfectly free. There was no one of them that spoke so much about liberty—a sound peculiarly pleasant to our ears—as the Apostle Paul; and he declares that we are called to it; that it is the very thing in religion to which we are called. Now, there is an apprehension, very wide-spread—and we can see how reasonably it has sprung up—that religion, so far from making men free, hampers them, restricts them, ties them up, burdens them; and there is among men a universal impression, when life is strong in young veins, and the impulse to do just as they wish to is power-

Preached at the TWIN MOUNTAIN HOUSE, White Mountains, N. H., Sunday morning, Sept. 13th, 1874. Lesson: Luke ix., 28-42. Hymns (Plymouth Collection): Nos. 31, 1166, "Doxology."

ful, that they do not want to be religious. The fact is that they want to enjoy themselves a little while.

They have a superabundance of hilarity, and a strong impulse toward enjoyment; and they think it will be time to be still and careful when the world is not so stimulating; they say, " When we are old enough to have the rheumatism, why, then we won't race and dance; when we don't want to laugh, why, then we'll be sober; and when we can't do anything else, then we'll get ready to die; but as long as we have vigor and vitality and sunlight and all sorts of pleasures, why, we're going to have a good time. We'll take the bad time when we can't help it." On the other hand, there are many persons—persons that are anxious about their children, and trying to bring them up well; people that take on the duty of instructing the community, and feel themselves responsible for what their fellow-men believe and what they do; folks that are trying to form and employ public sentiment—there are many such persons who are astonished when we say that religion is the freest of all things, that men who have once become converted and are truly Christians are no longer under the law, and that a typical Christian, one who is a type of what religion really should be, is a person that does just what he has a mind to. " A person that does what he has a mind to, a Christian?" say they: " why, it is contrary to the whole face of Scripture, which says that you must deny yourself; that you must take up your cross; that there must be a yoke and a burden. To preach that when a man becomes a true Christian he may do just what he has a mind to is flagitious, and will lead to licentiousness and all manner of self-indulgence." Historical developments are pointed to by men, of what are called "Antinomians," whom Christians have regarded as claiming to be raised to such a state that there was no more law for them, so that whenever they wanted to do a thing their doing it made the act right in their own estimation—the grace of God being given them to make them worse rather than better. Conservators of purity and religion are very much afraid of this doctrine of liberty, because they think it will break the bands of responsibility, and destroy the power of conscience upon men.

Now, Paul insists upon it that we are born to liberty, that we are called to liberty, and that the true typical Christian experience is one that takes away the power of the law over us, and gives us freedom to do what we want to do. Other inspired writers, and James among them, enjoin upon us the law of liberty, and exhort us to continue faithful therein, declaring that they are not unfruitful who do this. James says :

"Whoso looketh into the perfect law of liberty, and continueth therein, he being not a forgetful hearer, but a doer of the work, this man shall be blessed in his deed."

Men who are under the divine inspiration exhort us to liberty. How could this be if it were as flagitious in its results as men claim that it is ? Let us look into this matter a little.

What is liberty ? In the first place, the way in which men have learned to consider liberty has come from their experience in being oppressed by each other, and in emancipating themselves from the domination of a neighbor or a ruler. Breaking away from him has seemed to them to be liberty. In other words, the notion of being at liberty to do what you want to is intimately associated with the act of throwing off law and throwing off government. Men do not discriminate between the process by which one comes to a state of liberty and the essential element of that state.

In regard to civil liberty, we are very proud of having had the war of Independence. We broke away from Great Britain, and became masters of ourselves, and made our own laws, and elected our own officers; and as a nation we could do what we pleased without asking anybody's consent; and from these various historical developments of the power of liberty, men have come to hold the idea that liberty means ignoring authority and setting aside controlling laws.

Now, by your leave, I will say that no man is free until he is absolutely in bondage. No man is free until he is so in bondage that he does not know that he is in bondage. No man has true liberty until he has been so subdued that he accepts the control that is over him, and makes it his own, and ceases to be able to discriminate between his individual will and the law which is exterior to him. I think there will be no doubt about this matter if you will trace it step by step, and see how men are developed.

Consider, first, how men become, in their material and physical relations, large, strong, facile, and successful. When the child is born, and begins to learn the qualities of matter and the use of itself—of its feet, of its hands, of its eyes, and of its ears—what is the process by which we undertake to develop him out of weakness into strength? We teach him the knowledge of matter; we teach him what are the laws, as we say, of matter; and we teach him strictly to observe those laws. At first the child does not know the difference between cutting edges and blunt edges; but he learns it; and he learns how to accommodate himself to those qualities or natures. He does not know the difference between fire and ice, nor does he know the difference between water to be plunged into and the air to be breathed. He learns the peculiarities of these substances and their laws. No child has learned to go alone, to use his hands, and to have the comfort of his eye, of his ear, or of his mouth, until he has learned what are the laws to which these various organs must conform themselves; and learning on the part of the child is obeying; and obeying is coming to more of himself. Having his way by refusing law would be never to walk, never to use his hands, never to look, never to hear, never to taste, never to do anything except to have his own way, which would be to be an everlasting cipher or zero. Every step by which every child comes to be less and less a child and more and more of a man, every step by which he finds out more laws, on every side of him, in the air above, on the earth beneath, among men, in the infinite variety of the affairs of human life, is a step of obedience to law. He learns what laws are, and how to yield to them, and how to apply them; and he grows by compliance with them and obedience to them.

Follow it up a little. We educate ourselves either for pleasure or for accomplishment. How is it that one learns to become a pianist? By sitting down, and saying, "I am going to have my own way about this matter"—or, by finding out exactly what is required by the law of sound and by the law of instrumentation, and saying to the hand, "You have got to come to it: you don't like it, but you must come to it"; and twisting and turning, and twisting and turning it, and training and drilling, training and drilling it, through months and years? It will take a long time to subdue that hand to the nature of the instrument. It is going to control the instrument by-and-by; but it will control the instrument by-and-by because it has been a bond-slave to it. He who, having accepted the bondage of the instrument, drills his hand till it has become perfectly obedient to it, transfers to his hand all the virtue of that instrument.

The man who undertakes to play billiards must submit to law, and be led by it, until he has learned how to handle the cue, and how to strike the balls and make them rebound and affect each other. He cannot say, "I will do as I please here," until he is able to do just what the billiard table requires. When he has submitted himself to the nature of the game, and mastered its requirements, then he can say, "I will do as I have a mind to," because he is inclined to do what the laws of billiard playing demand.

So it is in regard to every single act of this sort—riding, fencing, dancing, rolling ten-pins, plowing, or cutting wood. In each of these instances the first step is the subjugation of yourself by obedience to the law; and the second, when you have obeyed it perfectly, is unconscious, automatic action. When you have reached this point you have perfect liberty—the power to go or to stop; to do or not to do; to accomplish in one way or in another. A man becomes large, facile, ingenious, accomplishing, in the proportion in which he has subjugated, by apprenticeship, every muscle, every nerve, every power, every element of his being, to the laws under which it acts. This denying of himself, this taking up his cross, in regard to all the specialties of life; this dying to himself and living in the laws that are around about him, gives him back to himself strong, wise, facile; and he becomes free in the proportion in which he has submitted himself to perfect training and drill.

That which is true in respect to the body is as true in respect to the social conditions of life. A man says, "I am born free and equal with all the world"; and in one sense all men are born free and equal. Men are said to be equal in our political bible; and politically men have equal rights—that is, they alike have the right to obey the laws, and to reap the fruits of obedience; and they have an equal right if they disobey the laws to be punished for it. The highest has an equal right to be punished with the lowest. In the eyes of the Government men are equal as citizens; they are equal before the law; but they are equal in no other sense. They are not equal in noses, nor in eyes, nor in ears, nor in any sense other than simply that of their fundamental political rights, which are, comparatively speaking, artificial and remote.

A man says, "I am born free, and am as good as anybody." It depends entirely upon who that *anybody* is. He says, "I do not believe in the laws of society, and I am going to do as I please." In that coarse sense he goes out into the community, and every single person is his enemy. A rude, vulgar man who goes into civilized society will find that all those among whom he moves are of necessity his antagonists; and he will be expelled from that society. A man who would move and thrive in the midst of refined and cultivated people must become acquainted with social laws, and must comply with them. When he begins to comply with them it is awkward for him. It is awkward for a man to come into a room gracefully when he has not learned the postures of polite society. He does not know what to do with his arms, nor how to stand or sit. What is an awkward man but a man who has not learned the laws of civility in the social relations of men to each other? There are such laws, although they are not written in a book. They are not penal laws, but they are laws which are just as real as though there was a penalty attached to them. The laws which govern one man in his intercourse with another in life are as real as those laws which govern the stellar universe. Every man who becomes facile and easy and natural in his relations to society becomes so because he has learned and complied with the conditions which are imposed upon him by society laws. It is by obedience that he comes to be free to do what he pleases. He is free to do what he pleases simply because he has learned how to please to do the things that are right, but on no other conditions.

That which is true in respect to social relations is as true in respect to civil relations. Who is the free man in society? Is it the counterfeiter, who watches with suspicion every man that knows him, and who is conscious that the whole armed force of society has been put, by his act, in battle array against him? The murderer, the thief, the gambler, has set at defiance the laws of society; and is he free? The man who is hunted, who is circumscribed, who is always in danger, and who has to create a circle for himself in order to exist at all, because society is his natural adversary—is he free? No. The man who is the most intelligent, and has the most perfect knowledge of the laws of the community, and believes them to be right, and so thoroughly obeys them that he does not know that he obeys them; the man who obeys laws and does not know it except when he begins—he is free.

When I am driving it does not occur to me that I am obeying any law. I turn to the right on the turnpike to avoid a stage that is likely to be run into by me, not because I think of the law that requires me to do so. I do it unconsciously. I do not go through the process of thinking, "I will turn out because I am required to by law." And after I have done it I do not think of it. When I bow to a man, I do it without thinking of it, and I do not treasure up the fact, and tell my wife about it when I go home. Having done it, I do not know that I did it. I speak kindly to a child, and give it sympathy, not because there is any law that says I must, (although there is such a law), but because when the law first said so to me I obeyed it so implicitly that I have forgotten it now. I perform the deed, not because public sentiment or law says, "Do it," but because I have been so drilled into it that I do it without law. The law says, "Thou shalt not steal;" but that is not why I refrain from stealing. The law does not permit me to do it; but if it did

I would n't. And now I do of myself that which the law once obliged me to do because I was so low and base and undeveloped that I needed something to show me what the best things were. I followed the law, I obeyed it, and finally I came to see, by my higher intelligence, what it was to be a true man; and this is the way to come to power and freedom.

That which is true in regard to social relations and civil matters is true in respect to political affairs. A man may be free under a despotism. That is to say, let the Czar of Russia issue his decrees so that every man knows just what he wants him to do, and let his subjects obey because they really believe theirs is the best government, and under it they become free. If they were always resisting it they would always be hedged in, hindered, restricted, bound; but by accepting it, though it be an imperfect administration, they become free in proportion as they conform to it, or in proportion as they run with those who are in sovereign power over them. In every government the man who accepts the law is the freest. The man who knows how to conform to the laws of commerce is freer than the man who does not know how to conform to them—for there are laws of commerce as much as there are laws of taste, laws of good manners, or any other laws that apply to the individual.

When a man first goes into business, he does not understand the laws which govern it, and we do not trust him with much liberty or scope. Why? Because he has not been trained to obedience to the inevitable and compulsory laws of commerce. When he has learned them, and is expert in them, and yields to them, and obeys them, we say of him, "He can go alone now." He has tied himself to those laws, and he has gone with them until they are incorporated into him and he into them; and he is free so far as he follows them; but if he resists them they restrict his liberty, and punish him.

So, liberty does not mean throwing off law: it means taking it on. Liberty does not mean opposing government: it means the most absolute submission to government, provided it is a right government, conformable to our bodily structure, our social make-up, our intellectual qualities, and our moral nature. He is freest who submits to the most laws, and submits to them the most implicity. No man gets possession of himself until he has gone through this process. The trouble and curse of daily life in every direction is the want of that unconscious or automatic action which is the result of training in laws and principles and obedience to them. Great mischief has come from men's imperfect knowledge of laws, and the imperfect manner in which they have submitted to them.

That which is true in respect to all our external relations you will find to be true in respect to our higher relations, or in respect to what is called, in distinction from our education in business, the education of our thoughts, our intellectual development, our philosophical elevation, our cultivation and refinement. In other words, when men are set to develop their mental faculties, they learn in just the same way that they do when they undertake to educate their muscles or their organs.

No man can learn to read except in one way. He cannot walk into a spelling-book and say, "I want r to have the force of t, and it shall." He must call r, r, and must give it the sound which custom gives it. M must be m to him, and b must be b to him. He must give to every letter in the alphabet the name and sound which belong to it. When a man begins to read he cannot say, "I will spell phthisic, t-i-s-i-c." Custom is law, and he is obliged to spell the word the other way—though I should not dare venture to tell you how! No man learns so simple a matter as reading or writing except by submitting himself to foregoing rules and regulations. Well, when a man begins to learn to read, he is exactly like folks who are just converted. "N-o, no; m-a-n, man; m-a-y, may; b-u-t, but; o-ff, off; t-h-e, the." Has the man who spells out his words thus learned to read? No. Why? Because he has to think of each letter in a word before he puts the letters together and pronounces the word. Do I do it? Do you do it? We do not. Why do we not? Because we have become so used to reading that our eye never sees a single letter in a word, nor a single word in a sentence. Indeed, we are not conscious of sentences even: we are only conscious of the ideas which are expressed by the sentences. Our minds are so drilled that we take in only the event or thing described by these symbols on paper. We see the history itself, the person himself, the occurrence itself; and the drama goes on before us as though we were looking through a glass at an actual picture.

Now, how do we come to that facility of reading? By familiarizing ourselves with instruments or letters until they become our servants, as we first become theirs. We bow ourselves down to these crooked symbols; and then we become so absolutely absorbed by them, in obedience to them, that they vanish and leave their power and effect in us as a part of our own personality.

The result is what we call "habit." Habit in the popular mind consists merely in doing things easily because we have become used to doing them; but it is more: it is really the augmentation of faculty. It is a new power which a man has gained by the repetition of acts until he has perfected himself in a given direction. It exalts him. It brings him upon a higher plane of cerebral power or capacity.

It may be said that no man knows a thing perfectly until it has become so much a part of himself that his knowledge of it and his use of it cease to be matters of consciousness. We cease to be conscious of the force of letters in a sentence, and yet we read; and just in proportion as we lose the consciousness of the letter-form we become perfect in the art of reading. No man knows how to walk well who thinks just how he is going to take every step. What is the trouble with awkward people when they go into company? Nobody is so graceful in things that belong to the farm as the farmer. If you bring him to Boston and ask him to go into conditions that he is not accustomed to, he is awkward; and the well-dressed, kid-gloved young man laughs to see how the poor old fellow acts; but now, take our young man and put him behind the plow, and see how he will act! He is as awkward there as the old man was in the city. But put the farmer behind the plow, and see the elasticity with which he adapts himself to its movements. He observes what is coming, and prepares for it, and goes along with the utmost ease and composure. Where a man has had education and drill in the thing to which he is appointed, and does it unconsciously and automatically, according to its kind, it is noble and beautiful.

When buildings are being constructed I sometimes am tempted to go up and see what they are, how they are made; and I observe that the first story I get up the ladder well enough; that the second story I hold a little tighter to the rounds; that the third story I lie flat against the ladder; that the fourth and fifth stories I tremble, and crawl like a worm; and that when I get to the top I very carefully place my foot on the gutter, or step on the platform, and scarcely dare look around; but I see the workmen—men that are not a bit smarter than I am—run up the ladder, step all over the roof, go everywhere, without stopping to look where they tread, climb a rafter, put two sticks together, and spring to the top of them, light as a bird, nimble as a squirrel, and sure-footed as a spider; and as I look at them I envy them. But I go up to-morrow, and find that I have a little more confidence, and am not quite so dizzy-headed. I go up the next day, and the next, and the next. The result is that by and by I can go up just as well as they can, and just as quick, and can do it without thinking what I am doing.

I remember that in Indianapolis I had a house built. I wanted to economize in every way I could, and meant to paint it myself; and I did. I got along well enough until I came to the gable end, which was two and a half stories high. When I began to paint there I was so afraid that I should fall off from the platform that I nearly rubbed out with my vest what I put on with the brush; but in the course of a week I got so used to climbing that I was as nimble as any painter in town.

No man has learned a lesson who thinks of it at all as a lesson. No man has learned a trade who has to stop and say, "How ought I to guide my hand?"

A man begins to set type in a printing office. Here is a composing stick, and here is a case of letters. He is told to set up, "All men are born free and equal," and he says to himself, "A. Where is A?" He looks for A, and finds it, feels of it and turns it over to get it in the right position. Then he says, "Double l," and he hunts for l; by and by he gets it, and puts it in the stick. At length he gets the first word set up; and finally the other words. But that man is not a printer, although he manages to set up "All men are free and equal." Go into the office of one of our dailies, and see a compositor set type there. He handles the letters so quick that your eye cannot follow them. His hand knows all about the case; it knows just where to find every letter; and no sooner does it touch the type than the type tells him which side up it is to go, without his thinking.

No person has learned anything so as to be perfect in it till he can do it without knowing it. When a man can do a thing without thinking of it, he has come to a state of liberty so far as that thing is concerned. He is in bondage to his notes who is obliged to think of his notes; he is in bondage to the piano who is obliged to think of the piano; but he is free who does not think of note or piano, and yet swells the strain and rolls off the symphony. He has subdued the music and the instrument; and now he may do what he pleases with them. He could only have done it, however, by going through what their laws required him to do, which lifted him to the capacity of doing.

All government in the family, all methods of civil government, all institutions of education and religion, ought to set this ideal before themselves. There is a great deal of government in the family that is mistaken. I have sometimes heard people say, "How poorly those boys have turned out! It is strange, too, because there never were boys more strictly brought up. To my certain knowledge, they used to be whipped once a week!" Yes, they were watched; they were kept out of evil; they were carefully instructed; and when they were of age, and went out of the family, they plunged into every liberty and every license, and proved themselves fallible and imperfect in every way. They learned a great many things in the family, but they never learned how to govern themselves. There are a great many fathers and mothers whose nature is to *govern*. The spirit of autocracy and monarchy is in them. They do not govern their children to teach those children to govern themselves, but they govern them for the sake of governing them; and they keep it up; and the children never learn self-government. Now, the object of governing a child is to get rid of the necessity of governing him. It is to teach him the use of his own faculties with regard to the great laws which are fundamental to you and him in common. If you bring up your children with a liberty which has restriction enough to make them obey the law, and with an amount of government which makes them independent and self-reliant, you will do that which is best for them. They will make blunders; but they will learn. They will fall into mistakes; but those mistakes will be a part of their training. You can bring up a child so that he is all compliance toward externality; but he will have no power in himself; and what will he be good for? He will be like dough, and will never amount to anything. These round, smooth folks, that come up so carefully, and that will roll in all ways with equal facility, and are of no particular account, serving as mere punctuation points to keep other folks apart, have not been well developed, or taught, or bred.

Power of knowledge, obedience, training until it becomes unconscious and automatic, is the end that is sought by the whole drift of divine government, as indicated by nature and revealed by the Gospel. It is not meant that we should go through this life acting as if the world were a life-boat, to be used merely for snatching as many folks from destruction as possible, and for taking them safely to heaven. This world is God's university or school, where men begin at zero, and are to unfold and come to manhood as the object of God's decrees and providence and grace, and of the common sense which God has given to us.

The whole drift of civil governments, of churches, of schools, and of families, should be to make men larger, bolder, more symmetrical, freer, and to do it by the way of discipline, drill, the knowledge of laws, and obedience to them.

I have conducted this subject thus far without considering

it specially in its application to morality and religion; but, after all, the end and drift of my discourse this morning is, *What does religion mean in a man?* The derivative meaning of the word *religion* is, To be bound; to be tied up as by allegiance; and the fulfillment of it, in a large part of the globe, has, unfortunately, been literal, and men have been *tied up.* The idea has been, very largely, that when a man became a Christian, he agreed with himself to give up dancing, and give up swearing, and give up gambling, and give up lying, and give up Sabbath-breaking, and give up dissipation, and give up bad company; and his creed, if he were to let it out, would be, "I will not do this, I will not do that, I will not do that, I will not do that," till by and by it will be as *knotty* as a pine plank sawn out of a small tree. Negatives are not to be derided nor despised; but a man who has nothing but negatives is a fool, and has no temperament, no vitality, no positiveness. The true religious man is a man who is positive and affirmative. A man who has nothing more than *nots* is nothing. To be anything he must have actual virtues.

A farmer goes to the agricultural fairs, next week or the week after; and he says, "I have a farm that I want to put in competition. It has not a weed on it—not one; it has not a Canada thistle; it has no purslain; it has not a dock; it has no plantain; it has not any mullein. There is not a weed on it, absolutely." "Well," it is asked him, "what are your crops?" "Oh, I—I—." "Have you any wheat?" "No." "Any corn?" "No." "Any grafts in the orchard?" "No; I have nothing of that kind—but I've got no weeds." And that is all!

There are a great many people who seem to think that religion means *not doing wrong.* As if a knitting machine would be considered good that never knit any stockings, because it never misknit! What is a man good for who simply does not do some things?

There are thousands of men that are bad who come nearer to the royal idea of manhood than many professed Christians, because they are positive, and do something—because they are not bladders filled with air—and because they are not dandelion blossoms, beautiful globes, worth nothing. A true man is a force-bearer and a force-producer. I understand that when a man becomes a Christian he has higher ideals, larger conceptions of life here and of the life to come. The motives which are addressed to him from the bosom of God are an inspiration by which he becomes more, does more, longs for more, strives for more, gains more. Before, he lived a circumscribed life; but now he moves out the walls on every side because he needs more room. "Lengthen thy cords, and strengthen thy stakes," is the right text for a true man. He that is a Christian ought to be a hundred times larger in every way than he was before he became a Christian. Larger in every way? Yes, larger in every way. What! larger in his passions? Yes, larger in his passions. His passions ought to be not only larger, but better and healthier. Pride ought to be stronger, only it ought to be in subjection to the law of love. It ought to be, under the influence of love, auxiliary to higher things, and not an autocrat in its own right. Every part of a man's nature is to be built up, and is to be made subordinate to love. Anything that God thought it worth while to put in a man, from his toe to his eyebrow, from the crown of his head to the sole of his foot, is worthy of our consideration. He has not employed anything in the making of you that will not be needed for fuel.

Take a great good-natured, jolly fellow, who sits on verandahs, and tells pleasant stories, and plays all sorts of games well, and is good at a pic-nic or a card party, and drinks a little too much wine. People say of him, "What a pity it is that he is not a Christian! He is in a dangerous way; and yet he is a capital man in many respects." He becomes a Christian, after having gone through certain proper exercises. He does not sit on verandahs any more. His thoughts no longer dwell on frivolous things. He does not laugh. He is not seen at card parties and pic-nics any more. He supposes these are wrong. What does he do? He goes to church, and to prayer-meetings, and is a devout worshiper; but he grows stupider and stupider all the time. Before he became a Christian he was a genial, good companion, but now he has cut that all off, and he does not take anything else on ; so that he really is weakened. To be sure, he may have withdrawn from certain faults ; but he has lost nearly as much in another direction as he has gained in this. I should say to such a man, It was not sociality, or gayety, or facility in amusement, that was your sin, but making such things the end and aim of your life. What you want to do is to make a complete manhood in Christ Jesus the end of your life, and take those lower things as instruments. Let every part of your nature, enlarged and made better, enter into that complete manhood. Taking Love as their supreme governor, let all the elements of your being, sweetened and made more powerful, aid in accomplishing this great work in the soul. A man ought to be better when he knows that he is living for that godliness which "is profitable unto all things, having promise of the life that now is, and of that which is to come." And yet, many persons come into the church from the world where they had strength and momentum in imperfect ways, and they lose that momentum and that strength because they do not understand that religion is not simply tying a man up, but tying him up to let him into a larger liberty. It drills him into obedience to law that he may be master of himself. No man is so free as that man who has accepted the law of God, which is expressed in the words, "Thou shalt love God supremely, and thy neighbor as thyself." There is no sound in the universe that cannot be chorded to that. Love is the only true concert-pitch. Let pride be the concert-pitch, and you cannot bring the orchestra of human nature into agreement with it. Let taste be the concert-pitch, and you cannot make all the other faculties of a man harmonize with it. There is many a part of our being with which all the other parts cannot be made concordant. But sound the word *love*—love to God and man—and there is no passion or appetite, there is no taste, there is no social feeling, there is no intellectual element, there is no moral sentiment, that cannot be brought into perfect accord with it—yea, and be made nobler and better by it.

He who understands that religion is the drilling of every part of his nature into accord with this great law of love by which God himself is bound, by which he governs, through which the world is ripening, and which is to fill the eternal heavens with blessedness—he that understands this, and accepts that law in earnest, and obeys it, day and night, in the field, in the shop, on the sea, everywhere, and making pride and vanity and selfishness subservient to love, trains himself in obedience to it till it is easier for him to be gracious and beneficent than anything else—he has become a man that has looked into the perfect law of liberty, and that is continuing therein. He has become a citizen of the commonwealth of the universe, and is absolutely free.

My Christian brethren, this is just what you need. I observe that many persons never settle anything. They never carry a battle to its final results. You are now fighting with pride, as you were twenty years ago, and you are fighting with your temper as you were twenty years ago; or, if there is any difference, it is because the fire of youth and early manhood has burned out in you. Grace has done nothing for you, and you have done little for yourselves. Many persons are just as avaricious, just as stingy, just as close-handed as they were when they began their Christian lives. They recognize it, and are sorry for it, and once in a while they shed impotent tears over it, and once in a while they offer a little resistance to it; but they do not say to the intractable faculty, "You shall come to this law of love, and you shall be trained and drilled till you obey it without flinching."

Here is a man who stands behind his counter. He is bilious and dyspeptic, and at home he is cross to his wife, and snappish to his children, and brutal to his inferiors; but when he goes into his store, where it is his interest to be complaisant, he is very agreeable. If a person comes in to buy something, he puts on, for the occasion, a commercial smile; but that is not benevolence—yes, it is benevolence just the same as moonshine is sunshine, cold, remote, reflected. Yet we are doing, in this, that and the other place, the same thing. We laugh at exaggerated instances of it, but we are not free from it ourselves.

We do not trust God. We are anxious with care. We fret and worry about to-day and to-morrow. We do not love our neighbor as ourselves. We are envious and jealous. We do not honor and prefer each other as we are commanded to. The welfare of man is not precious to us. Nothing pleases us so quick as a bad story told about somebody. There are persons who are ready to catch at criticisms, or anything suspicious about folks, and are never specially gratified at hearing anything good about them. Such persons have not fulfilled the law of love in these things. On the other hand there are persons who are always actuated by love, and are always glad to learn anything good, and sorry to learn anything evil, concerning their fellow-men. Love is their habitual disposition, morning, noon and night. They are always radiant and beaming, because their manifestation of love is automatic and unconscious. Where by education, by training and drill, the whole man is subdued by this power of divine and human love, one is a Christian.

You professed the Creed when you joined the church; but oh, that you would profess something higher than that which the Creed means! When you professed religion and joined the church you should have joined as a boy goes to school. Some seem to think that when a man joins the church he is like a celebrated portrait in a picture gallery, at which people point and say, "Governor So and So," or "Governor So and So." It is often thought that those inside the church are saints, and that those outside are sinners. It is no such thing. There are sinners inside as well as outside. Those that are inside are sinners under medication, and the others are sinners without medication. Those that are inside are sinners in a hospital, and the others are sinners in their own houses. As the term *sinner* is generally used in the community, it is a very misleading and misinterpreting notion that men have. A man is a sinner whether he is in the church or out of it. A Christian is a man who is attempting to subdue every part of his nature to the law of God. That law is Love to God and to men; and he who binds himself in slavery to it till he is perfectly subdued by it, till in its full strength it resides in him, and reigns there, and he rejoices, heaven rejoicing with him, in that victory by which he comes to a perfect liberty, is a Christian.

Oh, how narrow our views are of the power of God on the soul of man! Do you tell me that religion is failing because you see how bad a war is waged in the street where the desperate odds of business drive men hither and thither? Do you tell me that religion is failing because men in public and political life gain their positions through cunning and craft, and that only here and there one endures? Go with me to those places where the shadows that work grief and sorrow beat down on the household; go with me to the all-patient mother's side; go with me to her who is stripped of everything in life but her hope in God, and who is servant of all the neighborhood; go with me among the humble, and among the meek who shall inherit the earth, and you will find that there is a school where God, by the Holy Ghost, compels such obedience to the great law of love that persons rise up in simplicity and meekness, princes, kings, priests unto God, having the liberty of the realm, and do what they have a mind to because their whole soul has a mind to do the things which the law requires, and which God loves.

Such is the liberty that makes men free. He that is out of concord with those motions and throbs of the divine Heart that send currents of light through the universe is narrowing and dwarfing himself. He only is a full man who is a man in Christ Jesus.

PRAYER BEFORE THE SERMON.

DRAW near to us by thy Spirit, Almighty God and Heavenly Father, and make thyself known to our thoughts, not by display, as once thou didst upon the burning mountain, not by force, but by the inspiration of gentle thoughts and sweet affections, by relieving us from darkness, and sorrow, and fear, and remorse, and by breathing upon us peace, and gladness, and good will and hope. Draw us far away from animal life—from those that are around about us; from the bird, and from the insect, and from the beast; from all things that have but begun their lives; for we are thine, we are God's sons, and our true life is nearer to thee and to the invisible than to things seen and visible. Therefore may we know thy presence in the elevation of our souls; in the springing forth of joys to meet thee; and as the homeliest and lowliest things bear upon themselves tributes of joy in the morning wherein the sun beholds itself, and they are beautiful in his light, so may all our thoughts, joining in the light of thy rising glory, seem beautiful to thee; and may we reflect that thou art blessing us with thyself as nothing else in all the realm of the universe can bless us. May we realize that we are blest in thy love, in a conscious strength derived from thee, and in holy hopes born not of ourselves, though in us, but of thee.

Grant, we pray thee, that we may feel how much more we are than we seem to be, and how much less we are than we think ourselves to be. Grant that the things of which we boast, but which are poor, and perishing, may be revealed to us in their poverty, and the things which we neglect, wherein our true strength and our true greatness lie, may be revealed to us in their majesty and beauty; and that we may go out of our ordinary life, its servility, its bondage and its painfulness, into our higher life, where we shall be hid with Christ in God, in whom every one hath a covert and a refuge. We pray that this day God may become a name not of fear nor of authority alone, but of love and of joy. Wilt thou help every one to-day to roll away the stone, if he sit in darkness, and behold the risen Saviour. May Christ come forth this morning to every soul as the messenger and the symbol of hope in immortality. We pray that thou wilt help every soul to appropriate something from thee, O blessed Saviour, that it needs. Help every one who is conscious of deficiency, of ignorance, of short-comings, of perpetual transgressions, of wrongs done or permitted. Help each soul to lean upon thee, and to borrow of thee medicine, and food, and raiment, a staff for its weary feet, light for its eyes, hearing for its ears, and life for itself.

Be with all of us. Become to us the first and the last, the beginning and the end, the Alpha and Omega. Grant that we may have in thee that inheritance which we lack in ourselves.

We pray that thou wilt renew the joy that they have had whose joys have faded; that thou wilt redeem from sorrow those who are bent and ready to break; that thou wilt give strength to those that are weak; that thou wilt establish the feet of those that slide; that thou wilt deliver from their fears those that stand looking forth upon impending dangers; that thou wilt hush the anxieties of those that fret away the very fabric of life; that thou wilt still the tumult of passion in them that are bestead by passion; that thou wilt give control to those who are driven about by every wind of doctrine, and success to those who strive earnestly for that which is good, and are perpetually rolled back from it.

Grant to every one, this morning, according to his necessity. May those that hunger and thirst after righteousness be filled, and behold the Saviour who hath in him that which they need—who hath something that stands over against every want of the soul—who supplieth indeed the bread of life.

We pray that thou wilt grant to those who have known thee, and rejoice in thee, and dwell in peace from day to day, more manifestations of thyself, that they may every day come down from communion with God, as thy servant of old came down from the mountain, with a face shining with things spiritual, that men may behold and rejoice in the reflected light thereof; and that they may become ministers of peace, of salvation, and of hope to all that are around about them.

Grant, we pray thee, that we may have great joy of one another, to-day, as we dwell together for the hour. May we lay aside all the ugliness, and weakness, and pride, and envy, and jealousy, that so beset us in the world, and that separate us and make us so hurtful one to another. Grant that we may dwell in that peace which brings us nearer together. Grant that all the wrinkles which care has made may be smoothed out, that all trouble may be taken away, and that we may rejoice in each other as heirs of a common salvation, as children of a common parentage, and as pilgrims bound for a common blessedness in the land of immortality.

We pray that thy blessing may rest upon all that we love. Go to those that we have left behind; and visit those that have gone away from us and are upon the sea, or upon the land, in the city or in the wilderness, wherever they may be throughout the wide world.

O Lord, grant that thy blessing may be distilled as dew upon every heart in this presence. We pray that this may be an hour in which secret petitions shall go up and receive the pledges of answer and fulfillment from thee.

We pray that thou wilt bless this dwelling, and all that here control and manage. May the cause of God, the purity of the Holy Spirit, and the power of divine love, abide under this roof forever more. May all that have come up hither receive a blessing of God. May this be to them a day indeed of rest from evil, and of aspiration toward good.

Bless our whole land. Bring us more and more together in a true unity of reciprocal interests. May we be knit together in confidence, and in a desire for things that shall ennoble this whole nation.

We pray that intelligence may prevail everywhere. We pray that strength may be imparted to the weak. We pray that this great and prosperous nation, builded up by a thousand precious influences, may grow strong for justice, for goodness, for the rights of mankind, for peace and for prosperity throughout the whole world. And may the day speedily come when men shall love one another, and aid one another, and study the things which make for peace, and learn war no more; when there shall be no oppression known, nor any desire to oppress; when men shall be so strong that none can bind them; when the kingdom of God shall descend; and when the new heavens and the new earth in which dwelleth righteousness shall appear.

And to thy name shall be the praise, Father, Son, and Spirit, evermore. *Amen.*

PRAYER AFTER THE SERMON.

GRANT, we pray thee, dear Lord and Master, an incoming of light and knowledge that we may see more perfectly the truth; that we may know more perfectly that the way of Christ is the way of liberty; that we may understand that suffering means learning, and that tears betoken smiles, as from thorns come roses. Grant that we may comprehend how by submission we rule; how by obedience we come to a state in which we no longer need commands; how by conforming to law in our innermost man we rise higher than the law. Grant to every one in thy presence some portion of this truth, that he may order his life in accordance with it. May self-will die out, and may conformity to the will of God take the place of it, in the heart of every one here. May we try to be better in our families. May we seek to treat each other, in all the affairs of life, with more justice and more kindness. May we endeavor to apply the Gospel to our conduct. May it drive away doubt, and envy, and jealousy, and all the imps that Satan sends upon us. We pray that we may become children of the light, and that we may be children of the day, and walk in the full communion of freedom here, in the hope of a yet greater emancipation, and more perfect development in the world that is to come. O Lord, chide us for our narrowness. We are not hungry enough. We do not aspire enough. Our longings are too few and too easily satisfied. Give us more discontent. Grant that we may have more aspiration. Create in us a true hungering of the soul for that which is infinite and enduring. We ask it not for ourselves nor in our own wisdom, but in the adorable name of our Beloved, to whom, with the Father and the Holy Spirit, shall be praises everlasting. *Amen.*

V.
"AS A LITTLE CHILD."

"AS A LITTLE CHILD."

During the few weeks that I have been here, and have had the services of the Sabbath mornings under my charge, I have felt that both courtesy and good feeling required that, as far as possible, I should avoid all discussion and exposition that would raise questions of difference. Divided as the great Christian world is in various ways, internally and externally, into separate bands, it seems to me that the same courtesy should be employed when one stands in a promiscuous multitude in the community that is employed in the intercourse between families. In every neighborhood there are certain elements that are different in one family and another; and politeness requires that they should not interfere with each other's living. Every one is entitled to his own liberty; and there is a propriety in every other one respecting that liberty. I have undertaken, therefore, on the Sabbath mornings when I have spoken to you, to discuss those elements which were spiritually fundamental, and which belonged to all Christian sects in common—and I shall this morning do the same thing: for when you touch the question of true Christian experience; when you deal with the great subject of Christian character, all differences vanish. It will be found as you recede from the spiritual conception of manhood to the instruments by which men are educated that differences multiply and disputes increase; but as you go from the visible toward the invisible, and discuss the interior life of Christians, all differences gradually cease, and men come into perfect unity. If you could bring the whole great diverse brotherhood of Christians,

Preached at the TWIN MOUNTAIN HOUSE, Sept. 20, 1874. HYMNS: (Plymouth Collection) Nos. 776, 733, "Doxology."

under various names, together into a scene where all were lifted up to a holy enthusiasm in admiration for some great and noble deed, or in aspiration, you would find that they would take hold of hands together, and that there would be no separation. The essential element of Christianity *unites* men. Its instruments and external institutions *divide* them. Therefore he who speaks from the interior, and to the interior of Christian experience, speaks in accordance with the best judgments and the best aspirations of Christians of every sect.

In the 18th chapter of Matthew, and the opening verse, are the following words:

"At the same time came the disciples unto Jesus, saying, Who is the greatest in the kingdom of heaven?

That is very much, if you should put it in modern phrase, as if one should say, "What do you consider the most eminent state of Christian experience? What is your conception of the most perfect manhood?"

"And Jesus called a little child unto him, and set him in the midst of them, and said, Verily I say unto you, except ye be converted, and become as little children, ye shall not enter into the kingdom of heaven."

Let alone who is the greatest there;—you shall not even get in unless you become as little children.

"Whosoever, therefore, shall humble himself as this little child, the same is greatest in the kingdom of heaven."

We are to recollect that our Master stood at a time of the world when in various nations the ambition of manhood had been, or was, very strong. The Chaldean and the Assyrian had their conception of what was the most becoming in a man—they had their ideal heroes, in other words; the Greek had his ideal man and manhood; the Roman had very distinctly before his mind that which to him was the highest spectacle of manhood; the Jews, who were not one whit behind them, had clear conceptions of what was necessary to a perfect noble manhood; and our Master fell in with the universal disposition of men in their better moods, or of the best men in their better moods, to seek ideal perfection; and when they came to ask him, "Who is the greatest in the kingdom of heaven?"—that is, "What is the highest manhood?"—he took a little child and set him in their midst. And what was the signification of that?

The Master was surrounded by conceited men, whose ideal was so easily reached that there were tens of thousands in Jerusalem who had reached it, and who had gone, as they thought, as far as human nature could go; and perchance they were of those who said, "What lack I yet?" That was the spirit of the great mass of the best Jews. Their standard being so low, there were many elements that puffed them up; they felt that they knew a great deal; they had read the Old Testament—that is, the law of Moses, the prophets and the Psalms; their teachers had inspired them with the feeling that knowledge consisted in a minute rendering and an exact understanding of the distinctions of the exterior Mosaic law; they were very familiar with that; they therefore felt that there was scarcely anybody that could instruct them; and they were very proud and excessively conceited. Our Master stood in the midst of scribes, doctors, teachers, and eminent Jewish saints; and their feeling was, "We are ready to patronize you; we recognize that you are an able man, that you are a prophet, that you are one of us; and we will take you into our company if you will only disclose an *esprit de corps*. If you will go with us we will accept you." In their conceit they felt that they were orthodox, that they were saints; and Christ says to them, "If you wish to be eminent in the kingdom of heaven you must be converted—that is, you must be turned to just what you are not; you must empty yourselves all out of yourselves, and start over again; and you must be like little children."

Now, what is it in childhood that makes the model or conception of manhood? It is not that the child loves; it is not that the child is weak; it is not that the child is ignorant: it is that in childhood universally there is the impetus and aptitude to *learn*. It is not a sense of ignorance so much as an appetite for knowledge; and the whole force of the nature of the child, the whole impulse of the child's mind, is, "What is that? What is that? What is that?" and the child sits artlessly and receives what every one tells it. It is hungry for knowledge, and knowledge pours into it in ceaseless streams. But the Pharisees felt themselves to be like a bay into which the whole Atlantic ocean pours its tides, and fills it full, so that no more can be put into it without its running over ; and the Saviour said to them, "There is no man among you that knows anything about the kingdom of God. Such is your self-satisfied state that unless you be converted and become as children, unless you are conscious that you are profoundly ignorant, unless you have a different conception of what manhood means, and of the ways of obtaining it, and unless you become my scholars, and let me teach you the first elements of noble living, you shall not see the kingdom of heaven."

What, then, is "the kingdom of heaven"? It is an oriental figure ; and it is a figure which is better understood in a monarchy, and under a despotism, than in our democratic republican government. We have to form very artificial notions of it. But we are familiar with what is meant by a *cause*—the cause of temperance, the cause of virtue, the cause of truth ; we are familiar with what is meant by purity and justice, and so on ; and our knowledge of these things will help us somewhat to understand what our Master meant by "the kingdom of heaven."

The exact definition is given by the Apostle Paul, where he says, "The kingdom of God is not meat and drink [referring to the sacrificial rites and feasts of the Jews], but righteousness, [right-living, rectitude of life, in intent and endeavor], and peace [not blindness nor stupidity]." *Peace* does not mean the absence of disturbance. Peace is a positive quality. It is the highest condition in which correlated faculties can exist. It is intense tranquility. When the strongest feelings are in accord and all right, the highest excitement is the most peaceful state. All excitements that are painful or injurious are so because men are not perfect enough ; because they are not high enough ; because they do not average enough.

When you hear one of the noblest strains of Beethoven's symphonies, in ten or twelve different parts, it seems like one sound. Take those parts from each other, separate them, throw them against each other, and they agitate one another ;

but when they are perfectly concordant all the instruments swell together with their different natures. They are so related that their varying sounds become as one sound, and are completely harmonious.

When one feeling alone is excited, its excitement is disturbing, and the other feelings are in conflict; but when the whole mind is excited together, and concordantly, there is no disturbance, but all is peace. And that peace which is here meant is a peace of vitality: it is not a peace of stupidity or indifference. It is one of the noblest, highest, best and most comprehensive of feelings.

Then there is another element which the apostle mentions as belonging to the kingdom of heaven—namely, "joy in the Holy Ghost"—that is, inspired joy; that rapture which comes not from a sordid love of things which we can see or handle, but from the experience of those nobler hours, those supreme moments which are given to men; that ecstacy which comes from conscious communion, or from the unconscious possession of the highest feelings of our nature.

When, therefore, you put these elements together, and bring them into order, and weigh them, and interpret them in our familiar manner, the kingdom of God is simply the Realization of Manhood in the highest form. It begins on earth and terminates in heaven. He only is in the kingdom of God who has begun to develop in himself, with earnest purpose, all those qualities, that whole line of conduct, which is leading him toward the full idea of perfect manhood which God meant when he set up man.

Take a clock like that one in the office here, that never keeps time. What was it made for? To keep time. That was the design with which it was put together and set a-going. It may wander from the original purpose of its maker, and go too fast or too slow; nevertheless, that for which it was made was to register the lapse of time. That was the end which was contemplated in its construction. All clocks are made for that. It is what the man set out for who made it. He may have thought of selling it, and getting the money for it; but the constructive idea back of the commercial one was that it should register time. That is the root of the matter in every clock; and the clock is valuable in proportion as it does this, and worthless in proportion as it wanders from its maker's design.

Now, in the matter of manhood, the plenitude of reason, the fullness, richness, depth and power of the moral sentiments; the illumination that comes through the imagination; all those illusive graces that flash over the mind through fancy and mirth and humor; all those domestic affections which go where the mother-nature may not go in society relations; all those basilar forces which are indispensable to man in his warfare in the material world—all these elements (and how many there are of them! How easily they are put out of adjustment! How poorly they are constructed! How much they lack that training which shall lead them to work upward and in the right direction!)—all these elements constitute the conception of man, in full disclosure, with all his powers of mind and soul and spirit developed so that the whole being is one that obeys the laws of matter, social laws, intellectual laws, moral laws and spiritual laws.

Next, what is it to "*enter into* the kingdom of God"? In the first place, you want to throw away the idea of a city, of a gate, or of any material entering-in. Whoever undertakes to be a man according to the instruction of the word of God, though his ideal may not be complete, and undertakes to use himself so as to make himself better, and so as to grow more and more manly, has entered the kingdom of God.

Entering the kingdom of God, then, is entering a Christian, a higher and nobler, life. Entering the kingdom of God is being better. Meaning to be better systematically, as the end of one's life, is to enter the kingdom of God.

And what is being "converted"? It is *beginning* to do these things. What is it to be a farmer? Well, it is to obtain one's livelihood, or rather occupying one's time, in the cultivation of the soil. What is it to become converted from a minister to a farmer? It is to stop preaching much, and to go to work on a farm. It does not necessarily mean that I shall be a good farmer, or that I shall earn anything, or that I shall do my work in the best way, but that I shall devote my time to the business of farming. The moment I begin to devote myself to that business I begin to be a farmer.

What is it for a man who has been a liar all his life long to become a man of veracity? It is to set out with the purpose of fulfilling, as far as possible, the law of truth. It is hard for a man who has been living in an illusory world to get back into a world of realities; and it is hard for a man who has equivocated from his childhood up to speak the truth. No man speaks the truth easily who has not been trying to all his life, and still less one who has all his life indulged in falsehood. But when a man says, "I have been a liar; I see that lying is dishonorable and base; and I am going to try to be a man of truth," and makes a business of it for days and weeks and months, and means to keep on, he has begun to be a truthful man. He may yet falsify every day; but if, after all, he has his face set toward veracity, and toward overcoming the tendency to falsehood, and is growing in the belief of his neighbors, then he has begun to enter the kingdom of truth; he is a part of it; he is a disciple in it.

A man is taken sick. The physician says that morbific influences have a course that they must run; that when they have once started there is a tendency to keep on; and he will also tell you that by and by there comes a point where, under medication, or by the forces of nature, this tendency is exhausted, where it consummates itself, and where there begins to be a recuperative tendency. This man has been three weeks confined to his bed, and his physician says "The crisis is past; now there is a tendency to recovery." The man is "getting well"; he is "convalescent." But he is not well; his eyes are heavy; his bones ache; his organs do not perform their functions perfectly; he is on the "sick list" yet; it will be a long time before he will be on his feet; and when he is on his feet it will be a long time before he can make much use of himself; and after he commences to use himself it will be perhaps six months before he will be restored to full vigor and usefulness; and yet when the physician says, "The crisis is past," the man has begun to get well.

Now, to be converted means to set your face toward a

higher and nobler way of living—not to set yourself to do better according to the pattern of this neighborhood or according to the average public sentiment of the community; but to set yourself to do better according to the pattern of the highest manhood. The moment a man takes in a conception of his relations to God, of his eternal existence, of the change spiritual by which, by and by, he is to drop this mortal body and be associated with the general assembly and church of the first-born, and with the spirits of just men made perfect, in the other life; the moment a man comprehends the scope of his whole being here and hereafter, and says, "I am determined to live as a man should who has such a destiny in the life to come"—that moment he has entered into the kingdom of God.

We are stopped at this point by misconceptions widespread. In the first place, men say, "I understand by conversion a great change wrought in a man by which he passes from death to life, so that whereas yesterday he was a great sinner, to-day he is a child of grace; so that a man who is in the darkness of ignorance is immediately lifted into the light of truth, wherein everything becomes new to him." This impression is the more mischievous because it has a root of truth in it, a figurative expression being treated as though it were literal truth.

A man gets up in a conference meeting, a love-feast, or some church assembly, and says, "I was conscious that there was a great struggle in me against God and righteousness; and I was conscious of being suddenly led by the power of God so that everything seemed new to me. I never heard the birds sing so before. The world never seemed so beautiful to me before. I never before seemed to love everybody so. Everything appeared different. I was a new man. I was changed—completely changed." He really does feel as though he was completely changed. Well, is he? Let us see. He has been a stingy man. Is his stinginess quite dead? He has been a very proud man. The first effect of this spiritual shock that he has received was such that his head is not held so high, and his neck is a great deal more limber; but is his pride dead? You shall soon after hear him say, "We have our trials and troubles in the Christian life as elsewhere. I have had much light and comfort since I became a Christian; but I have had my ups and downs." What does he mean by "ups and downs"? He means that he was not completely changed by the Spirit of God. He *began* to be a Christian—that was the only change which he underwent. He simply started in the Christian course. His old habits were not burned up. There was a change; and pride, love of money, vanity, the affections, all the faculties of the mind, received an impulse in the right direction; but that impulse had not consolidated itself into fixed habits; and every man that is born into the kingdom of God, or converted, is merely started in the Christian life.

A man says, "I am going to emigrate. This is a poor country about the White Mountains; a man must be a stone to be contented to earn his living on these farms; I am going to Oregon, where the land is worth having;" but he cannot sell his farm; and he must look after his old mother, who cannot go; and he is hindered in various ways from carrying out his intention. He thinks about it much as many people think about becoming Christians. They want to be Christians; they never see any exhibition of Christian life, or witness any religious ceremony, that it does not stir them up and make them wish they were Christians; they feel that they must be Christians some time or other. By and by the mother dies, and the man says, "One string is broken that kept me here: now, if I can get rid of my farm, I will go." But there are vacillations in his mind. He says, "Can I get enough money to go with?" By and by he begins to read and think and inform himself. At length he sells his farm, and he has, perhaps, a thousand dollars; and he says, "What can I do with it?" He says at last, turning it over seriously in his mind, "I will go—I will go next Monday." Next Monday comes, and he starts. After traveling a day, he gets to Boston. An acquaintance meets him there, and says, "Hallo! I understood you were going to Oregon." "I am going there," says the man, "but I have not gone." Yes, he is going; but he is in New England yet; and when he has traveled another day he will be there still. He may stop in New York a week; but he is on his way to Oregon. When he is out of New York State and in the Western States he may wish to stop and see things there and make inquiries, but he is on his way to Oregon. He has begun his journey, although the comprehensive object for which he set out is not attained but is yet in a far distant land.

A man says, "I have been living a wicked life, without regard to the future, and now I am going to take a larger conception of manhood, to live for my Saviour, for eternity, for my own welfare here and hereafter, and for the honor and elevation of my fellow men." He surveys the matter and forms his purpose, and says, "I will, by the grace of God, undertake to live from this time forth by a higher rule and in a better way." *That man is converted.* How much is he converted? Well, he has started in the right way. But every subsequent day of his life he will find out that it is one thing to resolve, that it is another thing to execute, and that on entering upon a Christian life a man enters, not upon a course which by the omnipotent power of God has been shaved smooth and clean so that he rolls like a ball downhill easily all the time, but upon an education the most comprehensive and the most difficult that a man can conceive of.

When you have entered upon a Christian life you have undertaken, under all manner of circumstances and with every influence operating upon you, to take the forces of nature which are working incorrectly in you, and to take your understanding and moral sentiments and spiritual dispositions, and overrule them and control them so that you shall fulfill the great law of love to God and man.

Now, when a man begins such a work as that, he is like a boy that has gone to school. We are not further along, most of us, than such a one. The exceptions I shall have occasion to mention in a moment. The popular idea of a Christian is, that before he was a Christian he was a sinner—in other words, that he was a bag full of all sorts of weed-seeds, and that the Spirit of God came along and shook them up and emptied them out, and put the bag under a hopper, and filled it full of wheat, and tied it up, and set it in the church, where people point at it and say, "He is a Christian. He used to be a sinner full of vile seeds from bottom to top, but now he is all wheat." Men speak of persons in the church according to that false theory. They think that God has burned up all the chaff and straw, all that is inferior in them, and that they are filled with the Divine Spirit. Instead of that, Christ says to a man, "Would you be saved? Well, come after me, and let me teach you." That is the import of "Follow me" and "Become my disciple." *Disciple* simply means *scholar*. Christ is a school-master to us. We must learn in his kingdom divine ideas, and then we must practice them. We must be not only taught, but *trained* and *drilled*, in Christ's teaching, until it has become a part of our nature.

No man who is beginning to be a Christian is more than a beginner, or can be, in the very nature of the human mind; and when a man is converted—that is to say, when he has had a clear revelation of the enormity of sin, and he revolts from it, and turns away from it, and has a more or less vivid conception of the higher Christian life, and sets his face toward it, saying, "I believe that I am converted, and that I have entered into the kingdom of Christ"—he is like a little child, and has everthing to learn.

I make these explanations for a variety of reasons. First, many persons think, when they are converted, that they are perfect Christians. When a man has gone through conviction, and had an awful time, and wrestled with the Prince of Darkness, and he gets up in meeting, and says, "I remember that I could not eat my meals, that I tossed in bed two whole nights without sleep, and that when I knelt in prayer all seemed dark, till by and by I heard a voice, and peace came into my soul, and I shouted, 'Glory, glory, glory,'" people feel as though that experience showed that he had been rinsed and cleansed and scoured out, and that all in him that was bad was clean gone; but it is not so.

These dramatic experiences I do not in any way ridicule; but I smite them when they are misinterpreted so as to be mischievous, and I say to persons who, though they have them, are yet living a low life, "Do you not know that your conduct is inconsistent with your profession? Do you not know that you are constantly breaking your Christian vows? Do you not know that you are considered by those who are acquainted with you as no better than an infidel man, and that many who do not pretend to be Christians are regarded as more reliable than you?" They say: "Oh! well, you know that Christians sometimes backslide; but I have been converted, and I have the promises, and I am going to get into heaven." They think that from that dramatic experience which they went through when they were first converted, as they supposed, they are sure of being saved.

A man enters college and passes his examination, which is a pretty tough one, and is matriculated. But during term-time he does not study, but has his sprees and frolics, and does not make any preparation for the examination that is coming round; and when he is warned by his teachers and classmates, who say to him, "Look here, my friend, you are getting into trouble by not studying and preparing for the examination," he says, "I'd like to know if I'm not a member of the Freshman class. Haven't I been examined, and haven't I got in? Don't I belong to this college? I may be worse or better in the coming examination, but here I am in it." Yes, and he may be out of it when the examination comes!

"Many shall say unto him, Have we not prophesied in thy name, and in thy name done many wonderful works; and he shall profess unto them, I never knew you."

Men say, "Don't you know what a time I had when I was convicted and converted?" What does God care for that? The secret purpose of God is to make you *men*, and redeem you from animalism, and from the thrall and narrowness of pride and selfishness, and augment and enrich your nature, and *edify you*,—as the Scripture phrase is, build you up,—into resplendent, heroic manhood; and what boots it, under such circumstances, that you simply began to be a Christian? The question is, have you been built up?

I have seen in New York City, ten or twelve foundations for buildings where the cellar walls were started, and I have seen those cellar walls stand for six years, to my certain knowledge, without any superstructure built upon them. So I have seen many Christians converted who never got above the cellar walls. Nothing was ever built upon them. They never became perfect men in Christ Jesus.

We are converted, and have entered the kingdom of God, when we have become as little children, and have undertaken to be better men, according to our light and knowledge in every direction; when we have undertaken to educate ourselves in a better way of thinking, and feeling, and living; when we have undertaken to build up a better manhood: and it does not make any difference whether we come into the kingdom of God with uproar and a dramatic experience or not. If you are in the school of Christ and are faithful scholars, that is the main thing; and if you come in with bands playing and flags flying, and you are poor scholars, it will not do you any good that you have been converted and are in the church. You are to become as little children, in order that you may grow in grace. It is the attainment which you have made toward Christian manhood that is to measure your growth and determine the finality of your life and disposition.

But while on the one side I would expose these mistakes that men commit to their detriment, on the other side I make this exposition for the encouragement of thousands and thousands of persons who were instructed by Christian parents all through their childhood, and who have a substantial knowledge of the truth as it is laid down in Christian schemes, and who have strong yearnings and desires to live better, but who feel self-rebuked, and struggle in their minds. There are before me persons who have said, thousands of times, "I do feel as though, if I were only converted, I should like to live a Christian life." There are thousands who have wistfully looked on when father and mother or brothers and sisters have gone to partake of the Lord's Supper and said, "I wish I were worthy and could go; but I have never been converted. I do not belong to the church, and, therefore, the Lord's Supper is not for me."

Well, if you are standing and waiting for the Spirit of God instantly to catch you up, and strike light and heat through you, so as to transform you at once, then you are waiting upon an error; but it is possible for any one of you, at any moment, to be a Christian, now, here, before you leave your seat, while you are listening to me.

Suppose there were war again, and I were calling for soldiers, would you not become a soldier the moment you gave your name to me to be enrolled? Would you not consider yourself a soldier when you had separated from your friends and companions, and gone into the army, and signed your name, or given me leave to sign it for you? You would not be a soldier in one sense, but in another sense you would be. You would not have received any drill, but nevertheless you would have enlisted.

Now, it is not necessary that a man should be a whole Christian, it is not necessary that he should be educated in all the lore of Christ, in order to be a Christian. The moment he enters upon a Christian life he is like a child that has just entered a school. How does a child become a scholar? He enters the school as an abecedarian. He is not far along, to be sure; but he is beginning; and he is as really a scholar as he would be if he were further advanced in his education.

Suppose a child six years old on returning from school where he had just been received as a pupil should say, "Father, I am a scholar." And the father says, "If you are a scholar I will examine you;" and he takes down Newton's *Principia* and questions the child upon it. The father would show himself to be a fool in his idea of what constitutes a scholar. It is not to be supposed that a child in school would have that familiarity with an encyclopedia which belongs to the higher stages of development.

How much knowledge is it necessary that a man should have in order to begin to be a Christian? How much knowledge must a man have in order to begin to pray? He need not have any. The desire to pray is sufficient. That makes you like a little child. That was what you needed, and you have found it out; and the way to practice a Christian virtue is the way to show how very little you know. Let a man begin at any point in the Christian life with this thought: "I honestly mean to live according to the Christian pattern, the rule and law of Christ." What shall he do first? I do not care what he does first. Christ says, "If you give a cup of water in my name to a disciple, you shall not lose your reward." He says, "The kingdom of God is like a seed." What is a seed? It is an oak-tree in embryo. How much of an oak-tree is it? It is an acorn. This is planted; it is hidden. The first year it sprouts; and the second year it rises a little above the ground; but you will have to wait ten or fifteen or twenty years before it will give much shade; and it will be a hundred years before it becomes an acre-spreading tree.

Now, the kingdom of God in the soul of a man, according to the declaration of Christ, being like a seed, begins at the seminal form. It is a germ which grows. When one wishes to become a Christian man, and begins to act upon that wish, he is at most a seed, a germ, which must grow. You cannot, therefore, accept any doctrine of grace which says that by the Divine Spirit you shall be endowed with Christian excellences miraculously. You must begin at the bottom, and learn thing by thing, thing by thing, all the way through.

I am asked, "Suppose now, Mr. Beecher, one should come to you, in Brooklyn, on communion day, early in October, and say, 'I have been thinking of my past life, and I am not satisfied with it: my mind runs in too low a channel; my ideals are ignoble, base, worldly, and I have but an imperfect knowledge of the law of God, though so far as I can see it requires right living, and I am determined to attain it—may I partake of the Lord's Supper?'" I would say to him, "Yes, you may. Not that it is going to do you any miraculous good, but that it will produce an impression on your intellect and imagination." "May I join your church?" "Yes, if I have evidence that you are intelligent enough to know what you are doing, and if I perceive that you are determined, according to the best of your ability, to live a Christian life, and that you have begun it. Under such circumstances I will take you into my church as a child is taken into an academy." Is it asked, whether I require an examination? Yes, I do. I say to one applying for admission to a school, "If you do not know enough to enter the academy, you had better go into the primary school;" and I take him in, not because he is a perfect scholar, but because he wants to learn. And to a person applying for admission to the church, I open the door, and say, "Do you want to live a more manly life? Are you willing and determined to pattern your life on the ideal manhood as set forth by Christ Jesus?" If he gives affirmative answers to these questions, I say, "You had better come into the church, because the church is a place where we take men who are desirous of doing these things, and where they do them in little before they can do them in large."

If there is a person here who is discontented with his way of living, and wishes he could live a higher life, and can say, "I accept the ideal which is laid down in the Gospel, and will try to do better, taking Christ as my pattern," I regard him as a Christian—a Christian child. He is converted, and has become as a little child, and is ready to be further instructed.

Well, but, is not that a very loose and careless statement? Will not many unworthy persons say, "I have some virtues; I have enough stock to get into the church with." Will not people take advantage, and get into the church, and be satisfied with a superficial life, and undervalue the necessity of a deep moral subsoiling? I have no doubt that there may be such cases; but, on the other hand, in trying to keep them out, the view of the kingdom of God by which it is attempted to keep them out will also keep out many timid, sincere, sensitive persons. By such a course twenty will be hurt or hindered who ought to be in the church, where one is kept out who ought not to be there. I say, therefore, to the many young men and maidens here, You have a knowledge of what is expected of you; and if, having that knowledge, you have an impulse in the right direction, that is sufficient. Sufficient for what? Sufficient for *a leaven*, to begin with: not enough to end with (that comes by education), but enough to begin with. It is not only your duty, standing with the light of truth shining down upon you, to accept it and live in accordance with it; but it is your privilege to take your ground on that, and say, "I am willing to become a scholar, in order that I may become a full-grown man." And the mystery being all gone, why do not you begin to educate yourself?

Let me say, further, that many persons, as soon as they have gone into the church, are apt to feel as a person does who has insured his house. It may be burnt up, but it is insured, and he has a sense of security.

A man, going to Europe, may be sea-sick, and may not enjoy his voyage; but he says, "What matters it that I am miserable on the way? I shall soon be landed there, and then I shall feel all right." So, many persons regard the church as a life-boat designed to get men safely off from this world into heaven; and when they are in the church they feel safe. They say, "I may be a little poorer, I may be a little worse off than others in a worldly point of view; but being in the church I am secure, and shall go to heaven. My passage is all paid, my insurance is taken out, and nothing can interfere with my safety."

It is no such thing. The church is nothing in the world but simply an educating institution. A man may go to college and be a blockhead still. A man may enter upon a trade and be a bungler all his life. A man may go into the church and be coarse, and hard, and selfish, and proud, and vain, and not have at all the education that is adapted to a Christian life, or that it was intended to give him in the church.

Therefore, when a man goes into the church he goes there as a scholar goes into a school, or as an apprentice goes into a shop. He goes in for practice; he goes in to be taught; he goes in to learn a higher mode of life; and if we could get out of men's minds the idea that a sanctity comes from adhesion to the church, as if it were an equivalent for personal endeavor, for study, for labor, for conscientious responsibility, for yearning aspiration, for pressing forward, it would save them from much misconception, and from many mistakes. It is equivalent to nothing of the sort. It is a help toward these things. You may be better for being in the church, and you may be worse : if it helps you you are better, and if it hinders you you are worse.

A man is converted. He goes into the church, and joins himself to those who believe they are converted, and who are making a common endeavor to live aright. He says, after a week or ten days, "Look here, Parson, I guess you had better take my name off from that roll." "What is the matter?" says the parson. "Well, on such a night Jim and I quarreled, and I knocked him down, and I could not control my temper. There is no grace in my heart, or I never would have done that, although I do mean to live better. You had better take my name off." He is the very man that needs to be in the church.

Suppose, for instance, a man should say to a hotel keeper, in a terrific storm, at night, when the snow was blinding everybody, and when the wind was whirling everything about, "Look here! See how I am hurled about by the wind and storm. I'm not going into the hotel because I am not fit." That he is knocked and beat about is the very reason why he should go in.

And the fundamental condition on which you went into the church was that while you were under obligation to restrain your temper and conduct, and put hindrances in the way of your wrong-doing, nevertheless, you did not profess that your temper was completely under control. You went there to have it controlled. It got the better of you once, but that is no reason why you should not stay in the church. You knocked a man down ; but the experience connected with that event may have been a good lesson to him, or to you, or to both. You should learn from your mistakes. A man who does not know how to learn from his mistakes turns the best schoolmaster out of his life. We ought to profit from our follies and weaknesses and blunders.

You went into the church and got drunk. Well, you have been sober for six months—a thing which you could not have said during ten years before. The fact that you have improved should be an encouragement to you ; and the fact that you are not wholly reformed is a reason why you should remain among those who can aid you.

"We that are strong ought to bear the infirmities of the weak."

We are subject to the same temptations as our fellow men, and we are exhorted by the apostle to shield them and sympathize with them.

A man goes into the church to learn how to live Christianly. He does not say that he is perfect in any point. He is under instruction. He swears. It is not less than wrong. He ought to be ashamed of his swearing. His conscience ought to smite him. He ought to blush at the thought of it. But he ought not to consider all as lost because he has sworn. He should profit from that wickedness. If he deals with it wisely it may be wholesome to him, like tonic bitters to a man who is in a feeble state of health. It is a thing to be condemned, but it is no reason why he should say that he is not a Christian, or why he should not be one.

A man goes into the church. He is in business, and every man about him is actuated by selfishness, and resorts to adroitness, and is seeking his own interest; he is obliged to watch and guard against their avarice; and he says, "I have been sordid, hard, untruthful. There I did not exactly tell the truth. I am afraid I did make a slight misrepresentation there. A pretty fellow I am, pretending to be a Christian, and playing the hypocrite! I have not been sincere nor honest. I have lied; and how can a man who lies and equivocates call himself a Christian?" Well, do not you think there is need of his being one? and do not you think he has a conviction of sin of the right sort?—not that great generic conviction which men have when they measure themselves against God's law in a general way, but that specific conviction which a man has, when he says, "I am temptable in this faculty and in that; and my vanity and pride are leading me into temptation."

If, when you are beginning to find out the reality of your sickness, the doctor is called in, and he asks what your difficulty is, "Oh," you say, "I am a little unwell; I have a slight fever." He gives you a little cream of tartar, has your feet soaked, and directs that you shall be put to bed; but he does not know much about your case. The true way, when a man goes to his doctor, and represents himself as being sick, is for the doctor to take him one side, and inquire into his symptoms, and trace the disease to the vital organs, to the nerves, or to the muscles, and put his finger on the trouble, that he may know just what to do.

Now, in regard to a man who is attempting to be a Christian, it is a great deal better for him to know specifically where it is that he sins, and what power or passion or weak point it is that stands in his way. The incidental failures of men who are trying to be good are the very points where their convictions are practical, and where they have some validity. Aside from these their convictions are apt to be generic and imaginative, and of little practical force. You cannot, however, if you are proud, learn how to be humble in a day. You must not excuse yourself for the sins that you commit through pride, and say, "I am proud, and could not help it;" but if you find that you are proud, if you find that pride is organic in your nature, you are, in admitting its faults, to condemn yourself for them so far as it is in your power to prevent them; yet you are to recognize that it will require time to entirely correct them. It will take ten years to educate pride so that it shall work with benevolence; and to so educate it is a part of the business of being a Christian.

The mistake of many professed Christians is that of relying upon what they call their "hope." Many persons say that they are going to heaven because they have a hope. What is a hope? Suppose a snake should take its last year's skin, which it has cast off, and think it was bigger for that old dry skin? It would be very much like a Christian who takes what he calls his hope, that was never worth much, and that becomes less and less valuable the older it grows, and rests upon that. Many people talk in meetings about their hope, their hope, their hope,—but their hope is of no consequence if it is merely a thing of the past.

Now, the fact is, you are a scholar; and the question is, What have you learned? Are you stronger anywhere than you were? Are you better anywhere? Are you gaining, on the whole? Do you feel as though being a Christian was a business all over, outside and inside, touching life everywhere, so that you must needs, day by day, be lifted up and empowered by the help of God? If so, you are leading a true Christian life. If you can get help from the church, do so—the church was made to give help to such as you; but if you cannot get help from the church you are not obliged to go into the church. The church is not obligatory any more than Fulton Ferry is. I can refuse to cross the river on the ferry-boat, and say, "I won't pay the cent, or two cents: I am going to swim." I should have a right to swim if I preferred; but I should be a fool if I did. And if you say, "I do not want to join the church," you are under no obligation to join it. It was meant for your convenience and assistance; but if you think you can get along without it you are at perfect liberty to dispense with it. There is no obligation on any man to accept it. It is an overture of mercy, and not an overture of obligation, and is he wise who refuses it?

So, then, the kingdom of God consists in the actual existence of a superior manhood in men. Entering the kingdom of God is the beginning of education toward that superior manhood. No man can have the results of this education given to him at once. No man can overcome the tendencies that are in him immediately. It is not the office of the Divine Spirit to change a man from an imperfect to a perfect being by a direct command; it is the office of the Divine Spirit to *work* in a man to will and to do of the good pleasure of God, from day to day, leading him more and more into a perfect, completed manhood.

To be a Christian means to live right; to act according to the highest ideal of rectitude; to learn how, more and more, to carry one's self in obedience to the divine law; and he who does that may have great joy (that is a matter of temperament), or great sorrow (that also is a matter of temperament). He may have great struggles, partly because he does not understand himself, and partly because he does not understand those by whom he is surrounded; but he may be a Christian notwithstanding. And the evidence of this is not whether he is in the church or out of the church. The true evidence is a growth toward a nobler way of living, in thought and feeling—that is to be a man in Christ Jesus; and he that is trying to grow in that direction has a right to say, "If I persevere I shall by the grace of God be saved. I am not to be saved because I am so good, nor because I have attained so much. God's love saves me; but I must be salvable; I must be in a condition in which I can be saved; and I am passing more and more into that condition from day to day, and I hope at last to attain the blessedness of the heavenly rest."

Under these circumstances I wish to say to parents who are bringing up their children, that much of this work which is usually deferred until adult life may be accomplished in childhood. I think that children may often be brought up in the nurture and admonition of the Lord at an earlier age than it is commonly supposed that they can. But all children do not require the same training, and the results of training are not the same in all children. It is said, "If you bring up your children right when they are young, they will not depart from their right bringing up when they are old." That is true as a general rule, but suppose you take a child that has a bad father and a bad mother, whose fathers and mothers were also bad; suppose you take a child that has inherited through several generations accumulating tendencies toward the flesh and to evil? It is a very different thing to bring up that child right, from what it is to bring up a child right, whose parents were good people, and who has always been under the best moral influences.

You have the greatest difficulty in bringing your children up right, and the man over the way has no trouble with his. On the one hand he says, "I never used a whip on any of my children, and I never had more than once or twice to rebuke this girl. None of them are vicious, and all of them have respect for and are obedient to the law." On the other hand you say, "I try to bring up my children as his are brought up; but they are selfish, and jealous, and quarrelsome, and troublesome in every way, and I cannot do anything with them. I do not see why his grow up so well-behaved and mine do not." It is because your children are not his. Suppose a man that had wolves' cubs to bring up, should compare himself with another man that had lambs to bring up? It is one thing to bring up lambs, and another thing to bring up wolves' cubs.

Our children are of all sorts. If, however, they are taught from their earliest childhood their relation to God, to the other life, and to the nobilities of this life, and if they are *trained* as they are taught, it will be comparatively easy to bring them up right. But it will always be harder to bring up some children than others, because some are by their organic structure further away from God than others. You can bring all up so that the world will be better than if they had not been trained; but some can bring up their children with more ease than others.

Why should there be that difference? Ask God. I do not know. That is the way it works, and no man can tell why. The question for every man to ask is, "What is *my* duty? What is *my* privilege? What is *my* opportunity?" If God has given you children that are hard to bring up, it is your life business to bring them up, and you must accept it.

If your children are easy to bring up, you need not fret lest they will be mere moralists. Many people are concerned because their children are sweet, loving, and compliant, so that they cannot get an awful experience out of them. It is as if the bass viol should mourn because it cannot do what the flute does. It is as if the bass should complain because it is not like the tenor; the tenor because it is not like the alto; and the alto because it is not like the soprano. There is a difference between wind and stringed instruments, and there is a difference between the various parts of music; and there is just as much difference in human life between individuals.

Your children are susceptible of different degrees of education. They begin at different points in relation to moral perfection—some far away, and some much nearer; and that according to the great principle of heredity, as shown in the Old Testament. Every one must take his children where he finds them, and bring them up as best he can.

The point that I wish to make is this : that a child that

is brought up to seek truth and honesty and obedience, and that as he grows up to man's estate has these things presented to him, will find it easier to pass into the next higher stage of positive choice—of voluntary obedience, not to parents, but to God—than if he had not been rightly instructed. He will find it a world easier to enter upon a self-chosen life of higher consecration than if he had not been well brought up. If you say of a child that has been brought up well that he must be converted, I say that the transition in his case will be almost insensible and invisible, and that his instruction is right in analogy and runs parallel with adult life. It is a process by which he learns how to avoid evil and how to do good.

There are some who have always taught us that conversion is the work of the Holy Spirit, that without the Holy Spirit it is all an illusion, and that any other view tends to produce a sense of self-righteousness. I believe that as much as ever; but this also I believe: that when the Spirit of God acts, it acts according to the divine injunction,

"*Work out your own salvation* with fear and trembling, for it is God that worketh in you to will and to do of his good pleasure."

O Sun! bring me out violets and daisies from yonder sand-bank. For hundreds of years the sun has been shining on the desert sands of Sahara, and never has it produced a flower there; but in the meadow over against the house where my father brought me up, every year there were in the early spring an abundance of wild flowers. What is the difference between the shining of the sun on a sand heap and on loam? The loam is full of organic forms—full of seeds; and when the sun shines upon it, these seeds sprout and grow, and flowers, grass, etc., are the result; whereas, the sand is destitute of such organic forms, so that when the sun shines upon it no vegetation is the result. Where the soil is favorable, the sun's shining causes the plant to put forth a stem and throw down roots. Does it create those roots and that stem? No, it merely gives the stimulus which is necessary to their development. The preëxisting conditions are such that the stimulus which the sun gives is all that is needed to secure growth.

Now, in order to use the brain,—all the faculties, the reason, the affections, and the moral sentiments,—what we need is the stimulus of the divine Spirit. Then we use them according to great natural laws. God does not use them for us. He shines on us, and we use them. We are *workers together with God*, he giving the great generic stimulus by which our faculties develop, according to natural laws, the results which are required of us.

It takes nothing from the glory of God to have the world act as he made it to act, or to have mankind develop as he meant they should develop; and it is a hindrance to teach men to *wait* for that elapse of divine stimulus which is *every day* given to each one, and which needs only to be accepted to be enjoyed. If it is accepted in small things, it develops itself more and more, shining brighter and brighter unto the perfect day.

So then, my mission to you this morning is ended. My discourse is delivered, the drift of which is, that every man must needs be born at zero, and go up the scale; that every man must needs begin at the lowest point and develop upward and come to himself at the farther end of life. Nature does not lie at the point where men begin: it lies at the point where, with the best education, they end. It lies in that which we are capable of coming to—not in that primitive condition from which we came. My nature is not behind me: it is before me. It is what I can unfold into. That is my true self. Every living creature is competent to become better, wiser, stronger, nobler than he has been. It is for every one of you to enter that higher life, the kingdom of God; and you are to enter it not self-sufficient. If you enter the church, you are to enter it as little children, saying, "I need help, succor, inspiration." You are to enter it, if at all, that you may live better here and hereafter.

May God give you grace, every one of you, not to throw away even occasional good thoughts. They may not be sufficient to make up a perfect character; but they are sufficient to help you, and to enable you to help others. Do not despise the least things that tend or point in the right direction. If you but feel an impulse to live better in your neighborhood and to do something for those around about you, by improving the road, by repairing the sidewalk, by being public-spirited generally, cherish that impulse; strive to benefit your fellow-men. Be generous. Do not retail current slanders in the community. Study the things which make for peace. Have more pity for those who suffer. If the impulse of prayer comes to you; if your darlings are carried to the grave, or your wealth or honor is fading from you, and your whole soul is lifted up toward something you know not what, do not throw away this experience. There is nothing that lifts you from animalism and above this wicked world that you can afford to put your foot upon. If you wisely heed such things and augment them, they will lead you to those higher experiences out of which you shall see God.

Dearly beloved, we shall not meet again in the flesh. We go our several ways. May the dear love of Christ go with you all. You are beloved of Christ. My Father is your Father. My hope for heaven is your hope for heaven. In sickness, in discouragements, in disappointments, in sins, or in guilt, never give up hope in God. There is no other friend like him. Nobody loves you as he does. You do not know how to love and nourish your children with the tenderness and kindness with which God loves and nourishes you. You are rich as long as you have God. You are poor without him. And wherever you may go, my last words to you, who may never meet me again, are, Hope in God. Your hope, your salvation, is in him. *Hope in God!*

PRAYER BEFORE THE SERMON.

DRIVE away from before us, our Father, all clouds and darkness. Remember our ignorance and our weakness, and help us to lift up our thoughts in their better nature, and our feelings in their best estate, that we may bring to thee that with which thou art well pleased—our love and our gratitude. We rejoice that thou art made known to us through the household; and that those names which are dearest to us and most full of meaning, and that have never died out in all our memory, are the names of God. Thou art, blessed One, Father of every soul, whether he knows it or not. There is none that may not look up and say, Our Father. We rejoice that thou dost deal with us in affection, whether thou dost smile or dost frown; for whom thou lovest thou chastenest, and scourgest every son whom thou receivest. Thy chastisement is for our good, that we may be partakers of thy nature.

We pray that we may have faith to believe in the inheritance of the future. May we have confidence that our life is moving toward a land which is transcendent in all excellence, in plenitude of power, where, when we drop these mortal bodies we shall come forth into glorious realities which but faintly appear in this life. Grant that we may feel that we are living toward summer. As they that are in the far north, and wait in the darkness of winter, and rejoice to see its coming, when the sun shall again rise upon their horizon with light; so may we, wintered in time, look perpetually to death as sunrise; and may our departure hence be our emergence in the land of light. For what are we here, poorly instructed, full of prejudice, with mistake upon mistake, and sin upon sin, buffeted and tossed about hither and thither, by circumstances which are stronger than our will, often bent and biased? Behold, in our earthly estate, how imperfect we are, and how much of that which is at all good we owe, not to ourselves, not to the power of goodness in us, but to the influences which surround us in thy providence, and in the whole framework of life in society.

We beseech of thee, O Lord our God, since we are weak in all that is good, since we are so strong earthward, and so feeble heavenward, that thou wilt adjust thine administration over us according to our weakness and necessity through time. In the family the babes are most to us because they need most; and we should be most to thee if thou art our Father, because we are poor, and weak, and needy, and afar off. And this is the relation of God in Christ Jesus, blessed be thy name, that thou art a God of grace, capable of suffering for those that need some one to suffer for them; that thou art one that knows how to bear our burdens, and to carry our sorrows, and to make us better by receiving upon thine own self, in thy care and sympathy, and in thy nature, our troubles. Thou dost think, and wait, and labor, and mould, working in us to will and to do of thy good pleasure. We rejoice in this interpretation of a God adapted to the wants of men in this nascent state, just coming to intelligence, or just reaching forth out of intelligence into grace and moral beauty. We need longsuffering; we need infinite instruction; we need forgiveness and great compassion; and this thou art. Like as a father pitieth his children the Lord pitieth them that fear him. He knoweth our frame and remembereth that we are dust.

We bless thee, O God of all light, that thou art also the God of all comfort. Thou art infinitely perfect. We cannot ascend to the conception of such royalty as is in thee. We are afar off, seeing dimly, and feeling but intimations of what thou art, and of what thy glory is.

O Lord our God, we rejoice that thou wilt overflow and fill up every imperfect conception, and that thou wilt be infinitely better than any goodness that we ever thought of; infinitely more tender than any tenderness that we have ever known; infinitely more faithful than any fidelity that we have ever seen; infinitely more royal than any royalty that the earth has ever witnessed. How great is thy power and how great is thy wisdom must needs appear from the world that is without; but that which is thy power and thy wisdom, that which is thy glory, thy disposition, thy real life, thy pitying care, thy wonderful power of making happy those that are in thy household—who shall tell us of these things? When we come to see thee as thou art, and not as thou hast been framed to us as one that dwells in the external world; when we have dropped earth-born terms, and we behold thee in thine innermost being, all heaven will not contain thy glory. Then, all that are present, and we among them, must needs break forth into transports of gladness, and sing that new song which ascribes honor, and power, and glory unto thee. And still, and forever more, thou wilt lead us on, loving and beloved. More and more thou wilt develop the soul that is with thee, and prepare it for higher duties, for more glorious labors. We are sons of God, but it doth not yet appear what we shall be. We know not the meaning of it.. When our coronation comes, what the robe shall be, or the sceptre, or the harp, or the joy, or the employment, or the ways of life, we know not; but we know that thou wilt be exceeding abundantly more than we can conceive of here. It hath not entered into the heart of man to conceive of the glories that thou hast laid up for those who love thee.

We pray that we may have faith in these things even as those in winter have faith that the summer will come; or as those in the midst of storms know that sunshine will return. May we believe that the future is full of refinement, and intelligence, and purity, and fidelity, and all imaginable experiences of gladness and peace. which are not permitted to earth, and which men cannot receive here. In faith and in hope of the blessedness which is beyond may we be willing to bear the cross, and take upon ourselves burdens, and cares, and sorrows which scour our pride. May we be willing to be disciplined now, that by and by we may be lifted up into thine ethereal presence.

May we rejoice in that providence of God which knows all our wants and administers to all our necessities. Be pleased, we beseech of thee, to bless all who are in thy presence according to their circumstances. Grant thy blessing to those who are advanced in life, and drawing near to the overlooking mountain, and beholding afar off the promised land. May they, unlike thy servant of old, feel that their footsteps are going down to the Jordan, and that they shall pass over and behold the beauteous light of promise; and may the shining of the coming glory irradiate their faces before they pass out of our sight.

Look with compassion, we pray thee, upon those who are bearing the burdens of life. May they strive to serve thee in their daily duties, and endeavor in all things to be more and more conformed to the pattern of Jesus Christ. We pray that they may be diligent in business, and fervent in spirit, serving the Lord. May they resist temptations to sordidness, and selfishness, and pride, and all things that are unlovely. May they fight the good fight in the midst of their daily avocations, and so become more like God.

We pray that those who are advancing into the midst of the fierce experiences of mature life may find themselves confirmed in virtue, growing more and more steadfast, holding fast to their ideals of purity, and integrity, and truth, and justice. Let them never be ashamed of the heartswells and exultations which come from faith and hope, and the prospect of nobler living. And we pray that as they meet the storms and trials of life they may be as good soldiers who go forth amidst rejoicings and bannered display to the field of actual warfare, where with hardship and ten thousand forms of aggravated suffering they still maintain patriotism and manhood.

And may the young that go forth into the battle of life remember that thus they are to be made warriors and heroes. Wilt thou give them integrity and faith. May they believe in truth, in fidelity, in heroism, in the spirit land, in the presence of God, in the loving angels that surround them, in all things that are full of brightness, and hope, and promise. May they never become selfish. May they never cast themselves into the slough of worldliness. May they never be content with the husks that the swine eat. May the divine Spirit guide them in all their ways. May they have longings for things high and noble. May their lives not be disfigured by things low and gross. May they rise above temptations, and pursue the right ways. We pray that all their joys and hopes, all their sorrows and sadnesses, may be sanctified by the Spirit of God to prepare them for better living here and nobler triumphs hereafter.

Accept the thanksgiving of those who, this morning, desire to draw near with thank-offerings. How many instances come up before the minds of thy servants of thy sparing mercies, and of deliverances from impending dangers! How many parents think of their children dead, and are grateful to thee for thy kindness to them in the most trying exigences of their life! And we pray, if any come looking back upon children gone from them, or scattered throughout the world, that thou wilt sanctify to them their memory and their affection for them. If there are those whose children are about them, whom they are teaching, and on whose account they are often in great sorrow, and disappointment, and surprise, wilt thou grant that they may yet be steadfast, full of faith, and hold fast to the promises of God, and never despair. We pray, if there be those who are but beginning to present their children to the Lord, and who enter upon life with them, that they may feel this day the blessing of God resting upon them; and may their children become dearer to them because they are dear to God; and may they see upon their faces, not alone the light of earthly sweetness, but also the light of coming glory; and may they put more and more holy thoughts into the rearing of their offspring, and set them against the background of the eternal world so that they may shine upon them as stars shine from the other side; and may their children be brought up in all love, and with a nobler sense of rectitude than that with which they themselves were brought up.

We pray that thou wilt sanctify all our affections. May all our ways be directed in the light of that great undiscovered realm of the soul for which there is no language, where so much of our life passes, but where we have no communion and no fellowship. Sanctify the experiences of our life. Sanctify our silent sufferings. Sanctify all our aspirations, and hopes, and longings, and sorrows that come rolling, we know not how nor from whence, by celestial influences. Prepare us thus by joy and by sorrow, and measure thou both of them to us. Send us such schoolmasters as thou dost please, to make us better and better through our weakness and through our strength, until we are ripe; and then may the sickle flash and the reaper come, and may we go home with harvest songs sounding in our ears, garnered into the eternal heritage of our God.

And to the Father, the Son, and the Spirit shall be praises evermore. *Amen.*

PRAYER AFTER THE SERMON.

THOU best and most beloved in heaven, thou Father of all goodness and God of all grace and consolation, breathe upon the souls in this presence to make them discontented with themselves, discontented with their shortcomings, with their imperfections, with all that is wrong. Breathe hope into their hearts, that they may every one feel, in spite of all the past and its besetments, that there is for them a better life and a nobler manhood; breathe a spirit of tenderness into all that they may live together affianced in nobler friendship. We pray for the blessing of Almighty God upon every soul, upon all those that are dear to each one of us, upon all our households and all the consecrated hopes therein. We pray for our beloved land, and for all the nations of the earth. O Lord, how long? Behold the roaring misery of the world that groans and travails in pain; behold the fightings, the bloodshed, the terrible disasters and the speechless sufferings; behold around the globe how few know thee and how many are besotted. How long, O Lord, how long? Bring in the bright day when no man shall need to say to his neighbor, Know thou the Lord, but when every man shall know him from the greatest to the least. Cut short the time, make haste, thou that dwellest in the infinitude of strength, and bring to pass the latter-day glory when the new heaven and the new earth shall come in which dwelleth righteousness. And to thy name shall be the praise, forever and forever. *Amen.*

Services
OF
Morning Prayer.

I.

PAUL'S IDEA OF LOVE.

HYMN.

(PLYMOUTH COLLECTION, NO. 770.)

Must Jesus bear the cross alone,
   And all the world go free?
No, there's a cross for every one,
   And there's a cross for me.

How happy are the saints above,
   Who once went sorrowing here;
But now they taste unmingled love,
   And joy without a tear.

The consecrated cross I'll bear,
   Till death shall set me free,
And then go home my crown to wear—
   For there's a crown for me.

I.

PAUL'S IDEA OF LOVE.

SATURDAY MORNING, Sept. 5, 1874.

LESSON: 1 Cor. xiii.

In looking at the way in which the apostles preached Christ, we are very apt to seek for a mere literal, verbal, textual agreement between the Master and his disciples; but the spirit of Christ and the apostles is a great deal more remarkable than identity. Our Saviour never, under any circumstances, despised institutions, or laws, or usages; but he everywhere refused to make them idolatrous. He everywhere treated them as if they were subservient to the spiritual man, and to the spiritual wants of men. He never despised the Sabbath day; but when the Sabbath was so used that it oppressed men he condemned it, because man is more important than the Sabbath. He obeyed laws, recognized symbols, attended worship, observed rituals; and yet all these were, in his hands, made instruments for ministration to the inward wants of men.

Now came the apostles, preaching the new kingdom; but they did not break up the Jewish Church; they did not attack that church; they never went out of it; they lived and died in it; they gave their adhesion to all Jewish ideas, except when these came in conflict with the spiritual development of men; then, like their Master, they set them at naught and defied them. They gave themselves for man, and for man in his immortal part.

Thus, in the 12th of 1st Corinthians, Paul discusses all the physical phenomena that arose in the experience of the early Christians. The speaking of tongues, the working of miracles, the power of interpretation, gifts—of healing, of instructing, of witnessing, of every kind—these are all treated with respect and honor; and after he has gone through the whole he says, "Covet earnestly the best of all these gifts; and yet show I unto you a more excellent way." The church, its ordinances, its days of observance, its rituals, its government and its intellectual instruction, are all of them excellent, and some of them are better than others; and we ought to covet the best of them : yet, over against the church as a physical organization, and over against the instructing institutions of the church, I show you "a more excellent way." Well, what is that way? It is the development, in the individual heart and soul, of the great over-ruling law of beneficence and love.

"Though I speak with the tongues of men and of angels, and have not love, I am become as sounding brass or a tinkling cymbal."

By the love which is here spoken of ("charity" is a poor translation) is not meant personal attraction and personal inter-sphering, but that whole temper of mind in which one desires the good of all men, and yearns for them, and sympathizes with them. It is that state in which one soul is a benefaction to other souls, and in which its light is to men as is daylight to those who are weary of watching in the night.

"Though I have the gift of prophecy, and understand all mysteries, and all knowledge; and though I have all faith, so that I could remove mountains, and have not love, I am nothing. And though I bestow all my goods to feed the poor [as a kind of bribe to eternity to let me in finally], and though I give my body to be burned [as many and many a fanatic has done] and have not love, it profiteth me nothing."

Here are men going about and saying, "You must be agreed in doctrine; you must accept ordinances; you must observe rules and regulations; oh! this lax preaching will never do; you must have the foundations laid strong; you must see to it that you do not come short of the exact truth; you must take things as they have been handed down to you; for a systematic view of Christianity is indispensable;" but Paul rises up and says, "These are good for some things, but without love (which is the very thing that men do not teach or cultivate with anything like the earnestness they

PAUL'S IDEA OF LOVE. 139

bestow on their dogmas and forms, and which is not generally possessed) they are just nothing."

"Love suffereth long, and is kind; love envieth not; love vaunteth not itself, is not puffed up, doth not behave itself uncivilly [that is, it is polite], seeketh not her own, is not easily provoked, thinketh no evil; rejoiceth not in iniquity, but rejoiceth in the truth; beareth all things, believeth all things, hopeth all things, endureth all things. Love never faileth [it is not meant that love is never out of patience, but that it is one of those qualities which never waste away by the changes of time or the world]; but whether there be prophecies, they shall fail [because they belong to the mutable state]; whether there be tongues, they shall cease [they *have* ceased]; whether there be knowledge [that is, philosophy], it shall vanish away. For [and this is the reason] we know in part, and prophecy in part [truth is not wholly developed; we know it but in fragments; our best knowledge is only speculative]; but when that which is perfect is come, then that which is in part shall be done away."

To illustrate this, he says:

" When I was a child I spake as a child, I understood as a child, I thought as a child; but when I became a man I put away childish things."

It is as if he had said, "When I became a man, and looked on all the notions which I had when I was a little child, I laughed, and pushed them away as imperfect." And so men who in this world regard certain things as important, and are positive of them, and persecute each other about them, though they do not understand them except in spots —these men, in the other and higher life, will see that their proudest knowledge here was but shreds and patches. The ideas of spiritual things which we have in this world are poor and meager and imperfect, as compared with those which we will have in the other world.

"For now we see through a glass, darkly, but then face to face; now I know in part, but then shall I know even as also I am known. And now [as distinguished from these transient states that are relative to time and growth], *abideth* Faith, Hope, Love, these three; but the greatest of these is Love."

QUESTION: What is the meaning of "Believeth all things"?

MR. BEECHER : It means the aptitude of mind to accept everything that is good in others. There is one state of mind in which, when you present a favorable view of a person, people will look across to each other and wag their heads, as much as to say: "Oh! yes, you are shallow; you are taken in easily; there is a reason for all that; you do not suppose he is as good as he seems to be, do you?" There are some unbelieving people; but a true state of love tends to accept things for what they appear to be. Not that it is blind; not that it is easily hoodwinked; but its prevailing tendency is to believe good things of all people.

QUESTION: In conversation with a gentleman, I referred him to this chapter, and he said: "Don't you see that in this very chapter the passage, 'Believeth all things,' refers to the regular orthodox faith, and means that a man shall have a correct belief?"

MR. BEECHER: Well, the question of mere intellectual, speculate belief is settled here:

"Though I have the gift of prophecy, and understand all mysteries and all knowledge, and though I have *all* faith, and have not love, I am *nothing*."

What in New England we mean by orthodoxy, is a correct collocation of facts and ideas into a system of correct theology. Now, Paul says: "I do not despise these things at all; none of them are despicable; but if you have these things, and have not a glowing, burning feeling of love, they are absolutely worthless." People, however, cannot understand that a thing may be good if it is governed by a particular disposition, and worthless if it is not governed by that disposition.

To be sure that Paul is speaking of matters of disposition and not of belief, let us look at his phrases more in detail. Take the words which immediately precede these: "Doth not behave itself uncivilly." That passage refers to gentleness, embellished intercourse.

"Seeketh not her own," this means that love is disinterested in everything it does.

"Is not easily provoked"—that is, not quick-tempered, nor irritable. It does not go off at a flash.

"Thinketh no evil." This does not mean, thinketh no evil of itself, but thinketh no evil of others; is not prone to see the bad side.

"Rejoiceth not in iniquity." There is not a village or a neighborhood in which persons are not drawn, by a sort of epicurean relish, to where severe things are said, where people are discussed, and where, on the whole, the dark side of things is generally dwelt upon. There is a kind of zest which men have in thinking of others and finding fault with them, judging them critically, and discovering reasons for supposing that they are not quite so good as they make people believe they are, adding fact to fact as the basis of forming such a judgment, giving them an unfavorable portrait, and, on the whole, chewing that cud of thought about them which involves, more or less, the malign elements.

"Rejoiceth in the truth"—in things as they are at their best.

"Beareth all things." No matter what people do, no matter what they say, no matter how much they put upon you or put you about, the true spirit of love is sweet, and quiet, and takes all the vexatious part of social intercourse just as a traveler does the inconvenience which he meets on his way. He does not think of fighting the storm, or whining about it; he is in it, and he must go through it, so he makes up his mind to that, and does not complain. It is the same in disarranged domestic or neighborhood affairs. The true disposition bears what comes upon it under all circumstances.

"Believeth all things." The right spirit tends to believe all things. It does not believe with credulity; nevertheless, trust is its prevailing disposition.

Count Cavour, the ablest statesman in modern Europe, Bismarck not excepted, said one thing which, from a statesman's point of view, coincides with this deep interior life which Paul sets forth. He said, as the result of his experience, that he believed the man who trusted men would make fewer mistakes than the man who distrusted them. Diplomacy has always gone on the theory of distrusting everybody, according to the principle of the Italian Machiavelli; but the result of Count Cavour's experience, though he was an Italian, was just the contrary. "Love believeth all things;" and when the facts do not seem to square with belief it "hopeth all things;" and when hope fails it "endureth all things." It is like the sun, which carries healing to the hunchback, to the maimed, to the sick, and which pours its light and warmth on man, woman, and child everywhere. It is medicine for all, good and bad, strong and weak, high and low. Those that are bad it helps to be good, and those that are low it helps to rise, and hopes for them, and bears with them. Love is the all-healing divine spirit in the heart of man.

PRAYER.

Our Father, we thank thee that thou hast interpreted thyself to us, not by the voice of thy thunder, nor by thy lightning, nor by those great agencies of power which make us tremble, but have in them no sympathy and no compassion. Thou art to us as we are to our children. We love them not without chastisement, not without fear, not without the infliction of pain in discipline; and whom thou lovest thou chastenest, and thou dost scourge the sons whom thou receivest. Thou art our Father, and art most intimate, near, helpful, patient, full of all goodness. When we behold what thou didst work in thy servant on earth, when we behold the illumination which thou didst give to him, and the interpretation through him of the glory of the heart, and the realm and royalty of summer in the soul, we rejoice; but how much greater art thou than he! And how much beyond us is he!

We pray for the Spirit of God—not for inspiration, nor insight, nor wonder-working power, nor exaltation, nor rapture. We pray that we may have of that spirit which is in God, the Sufferer who lives to bear up the infant universe, and who, with the growing ages, is still the Burden Bearer, the Nurse, the Father. We pray that we may have that spirit which shall not demand that men shall serve and please us. As Christ pleased not himself, so may we please others, and not ourselves. We pray that we may in honor prefer one another. We pray that love may in us be a perpetual benefaction, an undying generosity, a constant beneficence, an endless power for good. May it not be in the experience of our moments of health and comfort that our affection is strong one for another. May love never fail with us. May it be the atmosphere which we breathe, in which we see, and through which the functions of our lives display themselves. May we be so caught into the innermost Spirit of God that there can be no Hell to us, and only Heaven—for where love is there is Heaven.

Forgive our sins, our selfishness, our pride, our vanity, our hastings, our strifes, and our heedlessness from which others suffer. Forgive the impatience and irritableness of our lives. Forgive our hopelessness and shortsightedness by which we see time-things and not the greater things that lie beyond.

Interpret to us each other. Interpret thyself to us by the daily events of our lives; by thy providence; by the great outward world in which we walk; and finally may we not see thee through these signs, and hints, and symbols, but may we behold thee as thou art, and know even as we are known. Then, in the ransomed state, with joy unutterable, we will cast our crowns and bow ourselves at thy feet, redeemed by love, and saved by love, forever and forever. *Amen.*

II.

THE VALUE OF MANKIND.

HYMN.

PLYMOUTH COLLECTION, NO. 823.

Walk in the light! so shalt thou know
  That fellowship of love
His Spirit only can bestow
  Who reigns in light above.

Walk in the light! and thou shalt find
  Thy heart made truly His,
Who dwells in cloudless light enshrined,
  In whom no darkness is.

Walk in the light! and thou shalt own
  Thy darkness passed away,
Because the Light has on thee shone
  In which is perfect day.

Walk in the light! and e'en the tomb
  No fearful shade shall wear;
Glory shall chase away its gloom,
  For Christ hath conquered there.

Walk in the light! thy path shall be
  Peaceful, serene and bright:
For God, by grace, shall dwell in thee,
  And God himself is light.

II.

THE VALUE OF MANKIND.

TUESDAY MORNING, Sept. 8, 1874.

I will read a few verses from the second chapter of Mark :
" And it came to pass, that, as Jesus sat at meat in his house [that is, in the house of the ruler who had entertained him], many publicans and sinners sat also together with Jesus and his disciples; for there were many, and they followed him."

As we learn from the other evangelists, he had been preaching in a most clear and convincing manner; and the moral sense of the great crowd, and especially of the more wicked and despised part of it, was profoundly stirred. It was one of those times when men were drawn to him,—for he had, evidently, hours when everybody seemed to be attached to him. He had lofty moods, moods of elevation, when all appeared to be afraid of him; but he also had moods that seemed to draw every one to him. One day, he was invited by one of the rulers to go and dine in his house. There was great enthusiasm among those that followed him. Many of them were outcasts. They were irreligious people. They were what the immoral classes are among us. Following him they were received in such a way, and his influence was such, that they sat down together with him and his disciples. That word *together* is very emphatic.

Everywhere, and in the East especially, the act of people eating together is as full of meaning as it can be. He that eats salt and bread under the roof of an Arab, or of one belonging to many of the old tribes, becomes sacred to him. Although among the Jews there was not the same simplicity which belonged to desert hospitality, yet that feeling was very strong among them.

Well, when Christ taught the publicans and sinners nobody said anything about that. When they thronged about him, and he showed them a little attention, the Pharisees began to murmur a little. When they sat down with him, and he ate bread with them, the Pharisees said unto his disciples, "How is it that he eateth and drinketh with publicans and sinners?" They could not understand that. There they stumbled.

Here was a young man who might have had a very admirable career; there was every opportunity open before him; but he was throwing himself away on this company; he was taking no pains about his influence; he was running over the sacredest feelings of the Jewish mind—for if there was anything more important than another to the Jews it was that they should not be defiled. They therefore scrupulously held themselves aloof from the unwashed and the low. It was about as much as a man's life was worth to break through the public opinion and do things that were proscribed; and that Christ should plunge right into this violation of the proprieties of his class and the moral sentiment of his church, was more than they could bear. It was carrying things to an extent which they could not stand.

You will observe that the Saviour did not do this for the sake of hurting anybody. He did not do it impudently or in a blazing way. It happened of itself, and he accepted it as it fell out; and his reply opened the whole view of the intent of his mission.

"When Jesus heard it [for when there is anything against a man there will always be somebody to come and tell him of it], he saith unto them, They that are whole have no need of the physician, but they that are sick. I came not to call the righteous [probably looking at the Pharisees], but sinners to repentance."

It is as if he had said, "I came from heaven with my God-nature, that wherever it went it should heal men, and not pain nor destroy them."

Healing may imply pain-inflicting; but it is pain inflicted not to exhibit or vindicate justice, or law, but helpfulness. The most magnificent vindication of rectitude is to bring a man back from wrong to right. If you can bring him back by tenderness and kindness, do it; but if you have to inflict pain, do that. To rectify a soul, to bring it to life and honor again, is the divinest act which is possible in this world.

It is at that point, I think, that our Roman notions constantly tend to override the spirit of domesticity which was the central spirit of Christ's kingdom. The vindication of law and public justice is essentially the Roman idea. What was regarded as the highest type of Roman character was hard, invincible, vindictive ; but in the mind of Jesus the noblest attribute of the soul was love, fulfilling righteousness, and bringing men back to repentance.

Then comes another case :

"And the disciples of John and of the Pharisees used to fast : and they come and say unto him, Why do the disciples of John and of the Pharisees fast, but thy disciples fast not?"

That is as if a rigorous Sunday-keeper should come into the family of an active, cheerful Christian man, and seeing that Sunday was a day on which they walked, and talked, and smiled, and laughed, and were joyous, and were deeply religious and very religiously active, should say to them, "I do not understand how it is that you can seem to be a good and happy man and so run over the Sabbath, not worshiping it nor observing it."

Now, fasting had become a kind of idolatrous usage. The Jews attached to it a certain value in itself. If a man is so inordinate an eater that he cannot really get through the clouds and come to religious ideas except by reducing his body through abstinence, it is a good thing for him to fast ; but if a man is all the time in the mood which men fast to produce, what is the use of his fasting ?

"And Jesus said unto them, Can the children of the bridechamber fast while the bridegroom is with them? As long as they have the bridegroom with them, they cannot fast. But the days will come when the bridegroom shall be taken away from them, and then shall they fast in those days."

It is a time of joy with them, and why should they make it a time of sorrow ? When it is a time of sorrow they will not want to eat and drink.

Then came a third instance :

"And it came to pass, that he went through the corn-fields on the

Sabbath-day; and his disciples began, as they went, to pluck the ears of corn. And the Pharisees said unto him, Behold, why do they on the Sabbath-day that which is not lawful?"

It was not lawful with them to work on the Sabbath day. It is not in our Puritan interpretation of the Bible lawful to do anything on Sunday, except to be sober, and worship, and so on; but the Jews made the Sabbath a cheerful day. Dinners, if cooked on Saturday, were perfectly lawful to be eaten in a festive way on Sunday. Hilarity after the religious services of the day was unquestionably admissible. But men must not work. That indicates one of the ways in which the Pharisees refined. They would say that a man must not walk on Sunday with a pair of shoes that had iron nails in them. Why? Because if, walking on the grass, the stroke of his feet should shell out the seeds from the grass-heads, it would be equivalent to threshing; and that would be work. Another example was this : they said, "You have a right to lead your horse to water if you take a short halter; but if you take a long halter you will have to carry it, and so you will work." There were a hundred such absurdities. Another was in regard to traveling on Sunday. Sometimes the good old saints would want to go out of the city and spend the day in the neighborhood. A Sabbath day's journey (the shortest of all journeys) was, among the Jews, a certain distance from one's home ; and the Jewish rabbis declared that a man's home was where he had set up rafters. And so if they wanted to leave the city on Sunday they would go and set up rafters within the distance of a Sabbath day's journey of the place where they wanted to go, and would call that a homestead, and then by going a Sabbath day's journey they would be where they wanted to go. They fixed the law very strict, and then dodged it. The land was full of such little crotchets of Pharisaic interpretation, and they became ridiculous.

But these particularities sprang from a noble source ; for when the Jews were carried away captive there was a likelihood that the Hebrews would intermarry, and that the people would become mixed. So the doctors began to interpret the law with new adaptations, and there were a thousand little peculiarities which were designed to separate the Jews from the heathen. The word *Pharisee* means separation. The design was to keep the Jews from mixing with the heathen. It was by that minute discipline that the Jews were held together, and brought back to the promised land; but in their new circumstances they did not spiritualize or liberalize. They stuck to these old peculiarities.

"He said unto them, Have ye never read what David did, when he had need, and was an hungered, he and they that were with him? how he went into the house of God in the days of Abiathar the high priest, and did eat the shew-bread, which was not lawful to eat but for the priests, and gave also to them that were with him?"

This illustration is exceedingly strong, because it was as near to sacrilege in the eyes of the people as it could possibly be. And Christ says, "Necessity of this kind knows no law." David took the shew-bread to save himself from starvation. The altar, the temple, and the bread were sacred in the eye of the law and were not to be profaned by ordinary and unconsecrated men; yet all of these sacred things were made for man's benefit; and when the royal leader of the whole people must save himself, is altar, or temple, or bread, or anything else as important as human life? Everything is to give way to manhood; that is the regnant element in human life; and no priest, nor church, nor ordinance, nor service, nor ceremony is so sacred that in his great emergencies man may not make them serve him. That was the doctrine that Christ taught. Manhood sprang from God; and all material conditions, all governments, all laws, all institutions, all usages in society must give way for its essential safety.

"And he said unto them, The Sabbath was made for man, and not man for the Sabbath; therefore, the Son of man is Lord also of the Sabbath."

PRAYER.

We thank thee, our Father, that we are permitted to bow down together, this morning, and call thee by that name which opens to us all the channels of remembrance, all the sweetness of our childhood. We thank thee for the love that was around about us in the family; and when we call thee "Father," we think likewise of our mother. We think of the days of blessedness, and peace, and trust, and rest, which we have had; and the heavens are benign, and the storms are all gone, and the light that abides with thee comes forth genial and warm—comforting us—for thou hast been proclaimed as a God of power, armed with the sword, till men look to behold the heavens scowling upon them. O Sun of righteousness, with healing in thy beams, break through the darkness that hath been spread over thee, and let men know that above every other place in the universe there is faith, and love, and yearning, and sympathy in the bosom of God. By as much as thou art better than we are, by so much dost thou transcend us in the power of loving, and in the healing power of love.

We pray that thou wilt so shine in upon us that we may understand thee by having something of thy nature incorporated in us, that the leaven of the divine soul may be in us, and abide in us, sweetening every out-going, tempering every passion, and giving hope and courage where there has been disobedience and infraction of thy law. May we not think of thee as a magistrate. May we scorn to think that we are walking on an exact line of law, and that unless we obey to the letter we are condemned. May we feel toward thee as, in its stumblings, and pettishness, and waywardness, the child feels toward its mother, in the arms of whose love it still looks for rescue and release. May we ever be near to thee in our bright hours of hope and joy, and nearest of all in our hours of darknsss, and despondency, and self-accusation. May we rise up against all temptations to evil, and may we know that all the burdens which the conscience bears are by reason of a lower manhood in us, and by reason of our adhesion to the physical and material world. And in proportion as we rise toward the nature of God, may we come into that state in which trust, and faith, and hope, and love shall abide in us; for they are of thee, and are like thee; and thine is that influence which is divine, which death shall not sweep away, and which shall grow in the other and brighter sphere, and perfect us.

Bless us, we pray thee, this morning and this day, and make it a peaceful and glad day. May we be helpful one to another, bearing each other's burdens. May we not rejoice in iniquity; may we rejoice, rather, in the truth; and in all things may we walk as disciples of Christ, pleasing him, and so being ourselves well pleased.

We ask these mercies in the adorable name of Jesus, to whom, with the Father and the Spirit, shall be praises everlasting. *Amen.*

III.

THE CHASTISEMENTS OF LOVE.

HYMN.

(PLYMOUTH COLLECTION, NO. 733.)

From every stormy wind that blows,
From every swelling tide of woes,
There is a calm, a sure retreat,
'Tis found beneath the mercy-seat.

There is a place where Jesus sheds
The oil of gladness on our heads,
A place of all on earth most sweet;
It is the blood-bought mercy-seat.

There is a scene where spirits blend,
Where friend holds fellowship with friend,
Though sundered far, by faith we meet
Around one common mercy-seat.

There, there on eagles wings we soar,
And sense and sin seem all no more;
And heaven comes down our souls to greet,
And glory crowns the mercy-seat.

Oh! let my hand forget her skill,
My tongue be silent, cold and still,
This throbbing heart forget to beat,
If I forget the mercy-seat.

III.

THE CHASTISEMENTS OF LOVE.

WEDNESDAY MORNING, Sept. 9, 1874.
LESSON: Heb. xii. 1-13.

I will read a portion of the 12th Chapter of the Book of Hebrews.

After mentioning, in the 11th Chapter, a long line of Jewish worthies who had by faith endured, and inherited the promises, mentioning all the names that were notable, the writer says:

"Wherefore, seeing we also are compassed about with so great a cloud of witnesses (such as those that he has been enumerating), let us lay aside every weight, and the sin which doth so easily beset us; and let us run with patience the race that is set before us."

They that are in trouble are certainly encouraged and comforted by looking back and seeing that others have been in the same trouble, and that they have by patient endurance overcome it. The writer, going through a whole gallery of pictures, pointing to these noble personages, says, "They all suffered, endured and gained victories; and let us run with patience the same race that they ran"—with this in addition, which they had not done:

"Looking unto Jesus, the author and finisher of our faith."

As "Alpha and Omega" (the first and last letters of the alphabet) are terms applied to Christ, as standing for all that is between them, and all that can be made out of them; as he is represented as the All in all; so we have him here spoken of as "the Author (the Beginner) and Finisher of our faith." The Saviour is presented to us in the light of One in whom our heart, our affection, our trust and our confidence may be absolutely buried, as a Person who is so large and worthy and noble that men love him with all their souls.

To the young mother, with her first child, there is nothing of sound or sight that happens which, in some way or other, is not connected with the child over which she has poured her life. She lives in that child. All her senses are absorbed in it.

There is a companionship of love, in which one absolutely includes another. It is that union of souls which is spoken of by our Master, where he says that we are to be one as he is one with the Father. There is such an absolute love of a man's soul that one is taken into another completely.

"Looking unto Jesus, the author and finisher of our faith; who, for the joy that was set before him, endured the cross, despising the shame, and is set down at the right hand of the throne of God."

There was his career, which had been in the beginning an argument of doubt and of fear, turned right about when better understood, and made to be an argument of strength and encouragement to all who are trying to live a Christian life.

"For consider him that endured such contradiction of sinners against himself, lest ye be wearied and faint in your minds."

That is the very trouble with which people meet. They get tired. They do not want to abruptly break away from their religious faith, or hope of immortality; but somehow they are spent; their mind refuses to come up to their purpose; day after day it gets more and more colorless; their faith leaks out; and they lose all vivid religious impressions.

"Ye have not resisted unto blood, striving against sin (as he did, and as did many of the worthies that are mentioned), and ye have forgotten the exhortation which speaketh unto you as unto children, My son, despise not thou the chastening of the Lord, nor faint when thou art rebuked of him; for whom the Lord loveth he chasteneth, and scourgeth every son whom he receiveth. If ye endure chastening, God dealeth with you as with sons; for what son is he whom the father chasteneth not? But if ye be without chastisement, whereof all are partakers, then are ye bastards, and not sons."

And now comes what would amount to the Jewish order of making a philosophical statement:

"Furthermore, we have had fathers of our flesh which corrected us, and we gave them reverence (we were not angry; on the other hand, we yielded obedience and reverential uplooking); shall we not much rather be in subjection unto the Father of spirits (as distinguished from the father of the body) and live? For they verily for a few days chastened us after their own pleasure (that is to say, for peace in the family, for their own comfort, and for the maintenance of their authority); but be for our profit, that we might be partakers of his holiness."

It is impossible for persons in life easily to answer the question, "Why was this sent upon me? What have I done? Why did I deserve to have my child taken away? Why was my property stripped from me? Why was I placed in such circumstances? What reason was there that I should be subjected to so much pain and suffering?" The question is not what you have done. God's dealing is not of the nature of a penal sentence at all: it is rather in the nature of a remedy. The question is, "What has he done this for? What use can I make of it? How can I make this trouble a schoolmaster to me? What part of my nature needs just this discipline? How shall I bear it in such a way that I shall become broader and stronger, or softer and sweeter and gentler?"

We are not therefore to look back upon our troubles; we are to look forward. They are material, they are instruments, that we are to fashion into a nature which shall be Christ in us, or such that, as it is here said, "we may be partakers of his holiness," so that the whole breadth of life everywhere, in secular work, social work, religious work, in youth, middle life, or old age, of every description, whether pleasurable or painful, are so many touches of that chisel in the hands of God by which he is shaping our features, and preparing to bring us forth into a form and beauty like his own.

"Wherefore lift up the hands which hang down, and the feeble knees; and make straight paths for your feet, lest that which is lame be turned out of the way; but let it rather be healed."

Paul is introducing a geographical picture of Palestine, in which were rocky paths over hills and through ravines; and he is also introducing, without mentioning it, the shepherd, who takes care of his flock, and chides them, and often strikes them, in order to bring them into the path, and save them from danger.

The fact of our trouble should be looked at in this large light—not in a way to overwhelm or destroy us, but in a way simply to strengthen our hands, and give us more courage to start afresh, strong, and to make straight paths for our feet, that the lame may not be turned out of the way, but may rather be healed.

Q.: Is there not a new element introduced in this command to make straight paths, that the lame be not turned out of the way? I think there is a certain allowance made for those that are lame. It seems to me that the design is to show that our lives are to be so ordered that these people, instead of being destroyed because they are lame, should be healed.

MR. BEECHER: Precisely. I hold that all offices of love and goodness are medicinal to those who are not lovely nor good. If putting them to pain will, in your kind intention and in your right spirit, help them, then put them to pain; but to put anybody to pain for wrong-doing, without any benefit to him or to those who are allied to him, is animal justice. Divine justice is to use pain, in the spirit of love, as a physician uses medicine, or as a surgeon uses the knife, always for healing.

REMARK: I think the office of divine justice is not only to heal or recall the individual evil-doer, but to have regard for the whole family, and consider how much they may suffer through him.

MR. BEECHER: Exactly as the father and mother have to consider all the six children when they are disciplining one; but the discipline of the one for the sake of the others does not mean the casting out of that one.

R.: It may be necessary to cast out the one for the sake of the others.

MR. BEECHER: That would be justified only in the extremest cases. One thing is certain, that the parent who will not cast out an erring child, but endures untold sufferings on his account, strikes us as the noblest.

R.: No, not when the other children are sacrificed by his misconduct.

MR. BEECHER: The effect produced by the spectacle of father and mother cheerfully giving their whole life in suffering for the reclamation of the one wayward child will be to lead the other children, as they come up, little by little to take hold and help; and so the whole family will be knitted together on a common ground in the common attempt to rescue him that is fallen.

R.: I am speaking of a case where one child is corrupting all the other children, and bringing them into antagonism to the parents, and breaking down their moral status. I think it is the duty of a parent, under such circumstances, to expose that child, and then separate him from the other children.

MR. BEECHER : I can see that it might be necessary that the erring child should be separated from the other children ; but I cannot see why under any circumstances it should be necessary that the parent should entirely break away from the child.

Q.: But suppose the child has set himself against the parent, suppose he has broken away from the parent, and suppose he is endeavoring to corrupt the other children?

MR. BEECHER : There is an element which you do not take into consideration—namely, that all parents work from the standpoint of weakness, while God works from the standpoint of everlasting power. Parents have to take things as they understand them ; and being feeble of understanding, though strong of heart, they are obliged to resort to expedients ; and one parent pursues a line of discipline that others would not, according to circumstances. Here is a poor woman, with twelve children, who goes out to work by the day. Her neighbors say, "It is better never to punish children corporally ; you ought always to reason with them, persuade them. Their wills ought to be educated." That is said by a dainty person who has but two children, four or five years apart, and has unbounded leisure to shield them and guide and direct them aright. But this poor woman, who does washing for a living, and sees her twelve children but once or twice a day, is obliged to use the capital with which she is endowed, and that is her right hand with a stick in it ; and although that is not the best way to bring them up, abstractly considered, it is the best way that she can bring them up.

Now, in respect to earthly parents, what is best to be done is always subordinated to the next thing—namely, What can these parents do ? What power have they ? Family government involves two elements : the need of the child and the competency of the parents—their will-power and their perseverance. We cannot reason from the weakness of men to the strength of God. Men are fallible and ignorant; but so far as God is concerned he has infinite resources. He never slumbers nor sleeps. He has all knowledge and all power. The universe is in his hand. Therefore any reasoning which is founded on human governments is misreasoning as applied to the divine government. I hold that there is but one theory of God's government in the universe that can justify an intelligent reverence and worship of God to those that think. If you choose to go on the ground of veneration, and take things as they are presented without analysis and reflection, that is well in its way; but if you undertake to justify the ways of God toward men, and present the theory of moral government, you must take the brotherhood of God and apply it to his relations with men here and hereafter, in the whole length and breadth of their existence. The true theory of the government of God is that it is a government of goodness established to overcome evil in the universe, to rectify that which is wrong, and to make the crooked straight.

R.: I should not have a doubt on that point if it were not for a doubt on another point—whether God is literally infinite in power. When we see that there was a man who lived in the bosom of Christ, who was his intimate friend, who was treated by him as a child when he was on earth, and who went away and sold his Saviour for a little money, it seems to us as though God had not supreme power over the human soul. It is said, "The light shineth in darkness, and the darkness comprehendeth it not." The light shone on Judas; Jesus held him in his arms, and loved him dearly; and Judas had not comprehension of Christ's nature. All he wanted was to make something out of the Saviour, when he thought he was going to have a kingdom; and when he found that he was not, he thought he would sell him for what he could get. He said to himself, "I will sell him to these men, and he will pass out of their hands again, unhurt, as on other occasions, and I will get the money, and he will get released." It would seem to show that with his great power, Christ, when he did all he could for Judas, could not save him.

MR. BEECHER: Well, this was not a plenary God. Those that hold the theory of the divinity of Christ believe that it was only the nature of God that could be exhibited by him, and not the full divine power; because he subjected himself to the conditions of limitation. That he endured Judas, knowing from the beginning what he was, and treated him as he treated the other disciples, and loved him as he loved them, is itself an indication of what I hold to be the general tenor of the divine government. That God interprets that government so is shown where he declares that he makes his sun to rise on the evil and on the good, and sends rain on the just and on the unjust; and where he recommends us to forgive our enemies, and to treat kindly those who despitefully use us, that we may become his children; thus basing his moral government on the general ground that whatever evil or aberration there is God is patient with it, and medicates it, and changes it as fast as it is susceptible of change, the primary object being recuperation, and not destruction.

R.: The history of Judas seems to indicate that there are some people who are incapable of understanding divine love, and that therefore they will be forever miserable.

MR. BEECHER: I cannot believe anything of the kind.

R.: I think the love is the same in either case.

MR. BEECHER: It carries you back to the thought that the moral Governor of the universe permits lower ignorant classes of men, without hindrance, to swarm upon the globe, and that they outnumber immeasurably the higher and intelligent classes. Consider the condition of the African and the Asiatic continents, to-day, where there are millions upon millions whose knowledge of moral truth is absolutely nothing. God has plenary power in the universe, and he permits this overwhelming tide to flow into the world and out of it again, year in and year out; and you must give some account of an administration that allows this and then damns these persons.

R.: He does not damn them: they do it themselves.

MR. BEECHER: Then he stands by and looks on.

R.: I mean people who have seen the good, who have known it, but who have resisted it.

MR. BEECHER: It is very doubtful to me whether there are such people.

R.: There seems to have been one—Judas.

MR. BEECHER: Well, he was not with Christ much over a year. We do not consider that if a child, after fifteen years of instruction by his parents, goes wrong, he is to be given up. Certainly not until they have expended their whole stock of moral influence upon him. They must have patience with him; and after they have borne with him twenty-five years, if he still holds out, it begins to be a serious matter.

R.: The Saviour says, "Have I not chosen you twelve, and one is a devil?" He viewed Judas, I think, judging from that expression, as very hopeless.

MR. BEECHER: So far as this life was concerned I think it was a pretty hopeless case; but Judas was not farther from understanding Christ than John was.

R.: I think he was.

MR. BEECHER: You recollect that when Christ was on his way to Jerusalem for the last time, and not long before his crucifixion, John wanted to call down fire from heaven upon the inhabitants of a Samaritan village because they would not receive Christ. If it was not a murderous and revengeful disposition that he manifested I do not know what would be. John had lain in his bosom, and was certainly the most susceptible to the interior nature of Christ of any of the disciples; and yet he had learned so little of that nature that when Christ was on his way to Jerusalem, for the last time, toward his crucifixion, he wanted these people destroyed because they slighted the Master. James and John, you know, were sons of thunder; and they showed it pretty much all the way through their lives by their impetuosity.

R.: Love is the most terrible thing in the world.

MR. BEECHER: Love with conscience and a good deal of combativeness is.

Now, to come back from this instructive but somewhat wandering conversation, the tenor of the whole passage here is this: that according to the theory propounded in this twelfth chapter of Hebrews, trouble is not necessarily penal. It may spring from an evolution of natural law, or social liability in connection with individuals and communities and nations. Comprehensively viewed, all our trouble is permitted to come upon us for the same reason that we put an instrument on a grindstone. In the one case the object is to sharpen the instrument, and in the other case the object is to profit us, to enlarge us, to strengthen us, to make us richer. Looked at as a whole, the divine government is a scheme of joy and sorrow. In other words, the use of every faculty of the human soul is to prepare men for a higher sphere, for exaltation, and finally for such a similarity to the divine nature that they shall worthily be called sons of God. And we, in contemplating that eternal work, should not only take courage, but should do everything in our power to help those who are weaker than we, so that the lame may not be turned aside, but healed.

In the time of Christ, the best men, according to the Jewish notion, the strictest, the most conscientious, and the most earnest religious people, were exceedingly proper, denying themselves every day, putting themselves to the utmost expense and care in order to live better lives than other folks; then they fell back on their goodness, and made it an imperative rule and measure, and criticised and condemned with scorn those who were poorer and weaker and wickeder than themselves; and it was against this that Christ hurled denunciations that seemed more merciless than any others that he ever uttered. The selfishness of the moral faculties he treated as being a great deal wickeder than all the passions and vices and crimes of the animal nature. The wickedness of the lower feelings is greater than we know or think; but the cruelty that men show in their thoughts and criticisms of their fellow men through the selfishness of their moral nature is more wicked still. Therefore, Christ said to the ruling class, "The publicans and harlots shall enter the kingdom of God before you."

PRAYER.

ALMIGHTY God, we pray that thou wilt give us light by which to live step by step. In the twilight of our career we are not yet born, but are struggling for life. We do not know how we are made. We do not understand the mystery of those inward forces that are every day propelling us. We do not know how to balance the strong parts against the weak parts of our nature. We do not understand to-morrow from to-day. We are children of the dust, and we bear our origin along with us. We are tempted; we are buffeted; we strive to maintain inward peace and rectitude of motive, and are assailed by storms from without, by sickness, and by a thousand troubles.

Now, thou knowest our frame, and thou rememberest that we are dust; and as a father pitieth his children, so the Lord pitieth them that fear him. We rejoice to believe that thou art a Highpriest that dost look upon all men to succor them, and that thou dost enter into the holy of holies, even into the heavens above, not to separate thyself from thy followers upon earth, but that in the secret places of power thou mayest send holy influences upon all that need. Thou art a high priest tempted in all points like as we are. No faculty in us is tried but that a like faculty in thee was tried, and thou knowest how to sympathize with our infirmities; and we rejoice to believe that thy providence is round about us; that thy thoughts are before us, and behind us, and over us, and that the care of no bird that flutters over her nest to feed her young, and the care of no mother who watches the cradle for her babe, is to be compared with God's tender care for us.

May we not distrust thee because thy movements are so vast and so voluminous, because they deal with such myriad creatures, and set the laws of nature to be nurses and school-masters fashioning them. May we not doubt thee because we misunderstand thee. May we still keep firm hold of the thought that God is all-bountiful, and lives, not to be himself happy, but to breathe happiness upon all his vast creation. And grant that we may cheer and comfort ourselves in the fear, and ignorance, and darkness, and perplexity of our minds, with the thought that as winter is constantly changing toward summer, so the soul may go from its winter toward the everlasting summer of God.

Strengthen us, we beseech of thee, in our personal difficulties; in temptations; in doubts; in trials; in our intercourse with the world; in fulfilling our duties among men; in everything that in thy wise providence thou hast decreed for us. Give us the inspiration of thy heart, and the sense of thy love. Give us trust in thee—implicit, overflowing trust—so that we may say, Though he slay me, yet will I trust him.

And so, being led thus day by day and year by year, at last may we stand, every one of us, in Zion and before God. And to the Father, the Son, and the Spirit, shall be praises evermore. *Amen.*

IV.
NEIGHBORLINESS.

HYMN.

(PLYMOUTH COLLECTION, NO. 424.)

Thou, O my Jesus, thou didst me
  Upon the cross embrace;
For me didst bear the nails and spear,
  And manifold disgrace.

And griefs and torments numberless,
  And sweat of agony,
Yea, death itself; and all for one
  That was Thine enemy.

Then why, O blessed Jesus Christ,
  Should I not love Thee well?
Not for the hope of winning heaven,
  Nor of escaping hell;

Not with the hope of gaining aught,
  Not seeking a reward;
But as thyself hast lovèd me,
  O ever-loving Lord.

E'en so I love Thee, and will love,
  And in thy praise will sing;
Solely because Thou art my God,
  And my eternal King.

IV.

NEIGHBORLINESS.

LESSON: Luke x. 25–37.

THURSDAY MORNING, *Sept.* 10, 1874.

"Behold a certain lawyer stood up and tempted him, saying, Master, what shall I do to inherit eternal life?"

The Jewish system combined civil and ecclesiastical polity, so that what are called "lawyers" in the New Testament do not answer to what we understand as lawyers in our time, but resemble far more nearly doctors of divinity who interpret the ecclesiastical or religious systems of the day. Scribes and doctors were men who interpreted both the civil and the religious laws, because these laws belonged to one system among the Jews.

"He said unto him, What is written in the law? how readest thou? And he, answering, said, Thou shalt love the Lord thy God with all thy heart, and with all thy soul, and with all thy strength, and with all thy mind; and thy neighbor as thyself. And he said unto him, Thou hast answered right; this do and thou shalt live."

The force of that is very much greater than we can imagine; because, unless you put yourself in the position, we will say, of a devotee in a church, who has been trained to think that every single thing which belongs to church organization is of tremendous importance and absolutely sacred, you cannot have any adequate conception of it. Take such a person, who has directions as to what he shall do at nine o'clock, at ten o'clock, at twelve o'clock, at two o'clock, at five o'clock, and at evening; who has prayers to recite for this and for that and for the other thing; who has enjoined upon him the observance of various ordinances and communions and confessions—take such a person, undiscriminating, who has been brought up surrounded by these external instruments, and has come to feel that they are almost like the direct inspiration of God's will to him, and tell him, "Now all these things are simply useless, or may be; if you simply have your thoughts seek God, that is all the worship he seeks or wants; Sundays, feast days, fast days, church services of every kind may be swept away, without any damage; worshiping God in your thoughts is the whole of worship"—and he is immeasurably shocked. But the Pharisees and Jews had hedged themselves about with an amount of service compared with which the extremest organizations of our day are very simple. Therefore, when the Jewish doctor, standing among filmy questions and casuistries, asked Christ, "What shall I do to inherit eternal life?" Christ asked him, "What is written in the law? How readest thou?"—in other words, "What are the commandments?" and he quotes this one: "Thou shalt love the Lord thy God," "and thy neighbor as thyself;" and Christ said, "Thou hast answered right: this do, and thou shalt live." It is as if the Saviour had said, "That is all you have to do; for the other things were designed, in their proper sphere, to enable you to do this. If you can do this, you may lay aside all external helps and instruments."

The answer, therefore, was much more weighty to the ears of the Pharisees and doctors than it is to our ears, at the first reading.

"But he, willing to justify himself, said unto Jesus, And who is my neighbor?" [instantly going on to one of the casuistical questions of his time.]

Now, instead of attempting to point out, with various refinements, who one's neighbor was, as an old rabbi would, Jesus began a fable:

"A certain man went down from Jerusalem to Jericho."

Evidently he was a good orthodox Jew; for he went to the right place. Jericho was peculiarly sacred. The way between the two places was a gorge, dark, and full of lurk'ng places; and it is notorious even now for being the resort of thieves and robbers. Well, this old Jew went down from Jerusalem to Jericho; and what happened to him?

"A certain man went down from Jerusalem to Jericho and fell

among thieves, which stripped him of his raiment, and wounded him, and departed, leaving him half dead."

The same thing happens to this hour.

"By chance there came a certain priest that way."

Priests, between duties in the assembly, went home to remain until the next term came on; and this one was going back to Jericho, which was his home.

"When he saw him, he passed by on the other side."

He made haste. He saw that there was trouble, and he did not want to know any more about it. He was going down toward home, but seeing the man at a distance, and fearing that he might get into some difficulty, he took pains to go on the other side, and passed by—as to this hour many persons do who do not want to make themselves acquainted with trouble; and avoid going where they know it is, and put themselves out of the way of it, so that they may not, in the natural course of their lives, come upon it.

"Likewise a Levite [a subordinate man in the temple—an underworker in the assembly], when he was at the place, came and looked on him."

And probably he said to himself, "Here is a case. I wonder where he's hit? He don't stir. I wonder if he is much hurt? Well, this *is* curious."

"And he passed by on the other side."

He was even harder than the priest. The priest was afraid to trust himself there; but the Levite came and looked him all over, and then went on the other side, and left him.

"But a certain Samaritan, as he journeyed, came where he was."

Now, if there was any creature in the world that was despicable in the eyes of an orthodox Jew, it was a Samaritan. There is no hatred like that of two persons in the same church, one of whom pretends to be a great deal higher and better than the other, but both of whom pretend to be the same thing. You will hardly find a church which has not in it a certain class that somebody thinks it is right to prey on. It seems almost necessary to human existence that men should have vent for their combative feelings. We must have somebody to kick and to damn; and the Jews had the Samaritans. We used to have the abolitionists; but we are now all at sea to know what class to select as the objects of our indignation. The Samaritans, however, were historically tough, and they endured to the end of the Jewish nation, so that the Jew never had any lack of something to hate. Our Lord, therefore, in selecting a Samaritan, and putting him in sharp contrast with the priest (the highest of the Jews), and the Levite (the official Jew), made the case as strong as it possibly could be. You cannot conceive of anything that would grate more harshly on a Jew's feelings than that.

"When he saw him he had compassion on him."

The priest had not, the Levite had not, but the detestable Samaritan had.

"And went to him, and bound up his wounds [imperiling himself by rendering himself liable to be assaulted and set upon by the same band of thieves, but caring nothing for his own danger], pouring in oil and wine [the oil in his wounds and the wine in his mouth, I suppose], and set him on his own beast, and brought him to an inn, and took care of him. And on the morrow, when he departed, he took out two pence, and gave them to the host, and said unto him, Take care of him; and whatever thou spendest more, when I come again I will repay thee."

He followed him up. He did not let him go. He made a thorough business of it. Having put him on his beast, he took him to a tavern, which was at a considerable distance, and gave orders to have him taken care of. The next day, having seen him made comfortable, and being sure that he was on the way to recovery, he thought of the future, and took out two pence (which gives us a very different idea of taverns from what we have now), and gave them to the host, and told him whatever more was required to supply the man's wants he would pay on his return.

Of all men on earth the Samaritan was the man who had a right to be careless of what became of a Jew, who was his sworn enemy; but while the best of the Jews refused the offices of humanity, the Samaritan, contrary to the human feeling and national impulse, took care of the unfortunate victim at his own peril and expense, and would not give him up till with labor and trouble he had brought him to a safe place, and watched over him until he was cured.

All that is painted by the hand of a master. There is not a word squandered.

"Which now, of these three [says the Master, lifting himself up, and looking in the eye of the finikin doctor of the law], thinkest thou was neighbor unto him that fell among the thieves?"

An honest man would have said, "The Samaritan"; but he dodged that word.

"And he said, He that showed mercy on him [by that periphrasis going around the hated name]. Then said Jesus unto him, Go and do thou likewise."

It is not enough for us to stand and watch how Christ hit the mark, as one would stand at a rifle-shooting and see how each man hit the mark. It was given for our instruction throughout the world, throughout all time; it is an interpretation of the law of kindness which fell from the lips of our Master, and it belongs to our every-day life. There is nothing that lives that is not the subject of this law. You might expand the bounds beyond the human family, and include the whole animal creation, and there would be nothing susceptible of suffering to which we would not be related. There is no trouble of any inanimate creature that ought not to be your trouble, if you are in the vicinity of it; and you have no right to excuse yourself from relieving it because it is not of your household, your class or your nationality. Man belongs to man, the world over. No matter what divisions there may be in society, and no matter how necessary they may be, the moment the question of humanity comes up all men are members one of another, and there is no reason why one should draw back from another on any ground whatsoever.

PRAYER.

Our Heavenly Father, wilt thou shine down upon our hearts with that light which makes our day; for not when the sun shines alone is it day if there be darkness in us. If there be the night of despondency, or of unbelief, or of angry passions, lowering like clouds over the day, then it is not day unto us. Only in the light of thy countenance do we see light. We pray for that communication of thyself that shall arouse in us that which is like thee, and give it ascendency, so that all our sky above us may be bright, as the earthly heaven is bright with the light of the sun; and in that light may we behold all things in their true colors and proportions. May we be exalted above mere animal rules, and our physical position in the world. May we think of ourselves as the sons of God, belonging to another and higher kingdom, with better laws, and impulses, and influences, and treasures that the world knows nothing of—holy thoughts, peaceful feelings, deep loves, and rejoicings of the innermost soul.

Grant, we pray thee, that we may walk, this day, as they have a right to walk who are the sons of God, ordained by no outward touch, sent forth of God among men, known of God, beloved of him, and sustained by his power. Grant that we may go whither we are called, with contentment and with a resignation to thy will. For what is all time, and the round world, compared with one thought of thine? What are all the issues of life but shadows, but passing things, that quench themselves as a taper is quenched at night? The long day of life itself—how short is it when measured upon the cycles of the eternal world!

Lift us up, we beseech of thee. As they that ascend the mountain are lifted above many and many clouds below, and can look down upon them, so may we look down upon care, and discontent, and anxiety, and troubles, and storms in life. Give us such life in thee that we may have dominion over ourselves and over our circumstances. Give us patience to wait. Give us courage to contend. Give us endurance to bear burdens. May we be able to take the scorching of the sun by day, and may we also take the darkness and solitariness of the night, and be found adequate everywhere and always to the calls and demands of God's providence. May we not be concerned nor troubled about trifles. May we not be led to fret, nor to wear out our joy by petty cares. May we have rest in God; and not only may we have enough for our own peace, but may we have enough so that we can impart peacefulness to the troubled, and calm their disquieted moments.

Give us this fellowship of the spirit, this noble friendship, this forward-looking, this faith of the Gospel which rests in immortality. May we taste beforehand some of those joys which we are to inherit. Bless each according to his want, and according to the wants of those who are dearest to him. And thus wilt thou carry us on from day to day until the welcome word shall come, You are needed in your Father's house; and with joy unspeakable may we rise, and go forth, and fly to that land where is no more winter, no more sorrow, no more endurance, but high and sacred joy, for evermore. *Amen.*

V.
ḤEAVEN.

HYMN.

(PLYMOUTH COLLECTION, NO. 545.)

Awake, my soul, in joyful lays,
And sing thy great Redeemer's praise;
He justly claims a song for me,
His loving-kindness, O how free!

When trouble, like a gloomy cloud,
Has gathered thick and thundered loud,
He near my soul has always stood,
His loving-kindness, O how good!

Often I feel my sinful heart
Prone from my Jesus to depart;
But though I have him oft forgot,
His loving-kindness changes not.

Soon shall I pass the gloomy vale,
Soon all my mortal powers must fail;
O may my last expiring breath,
His loving-kindness sing in death.

Then let me mount and soar away
To the bright world of endless day;
And sing with rapture and surprise,
His loving kindness in the skies.

V.

HEAVEN.

LESSON: Heb. xii. 18-29. FRIDAY MORNING, *Sept.* 11, 1874.

"For ye are not come unto the mount that might be touched, and that burned with fire, nor unto blackness, and darkness, and tempest, and the sound of a trumpet, and the voice of words."

This is a description of the future, and of the great aërial and spiritual band. Their life was all moving. It is the heavenly land that is spoken of. And you will take notice that in writing to the Hebrews the writer gathered together all those themes which lay within the knowledge of the Hebrew patriot. His love of country, his love of industry, all the historical elements that he was proud of, and the various topographical elements that are so strong in the imagination and memory of men—these were employed by him. But we have only a secondary and artificial relation to them.

There are two ways in which we can construe such a description as this. One is the literal way, attempting to make believe that we are Jews, or that we feel now what they used to feel. The other is an emulation of the spirit of it, exercising the liberty which we have of doing by our race-stock, and by our habits of life, what the apostle does here by the Jewish habits of life and race-stock. We have a right to construct a heaven out of the things which have been given to us on earth, provided it can be done on the higher spiritual plane. Everybody has in his own life some things which are so dear that if he could put them forward and imagine a land in which these were familiar things it would give reality and sweetness to it. And I think we have exactly that right. I think this is addressed to our imagination as it was to the Jewish imagination.

"Ye are not come to the mount [evidently Mount Sinai, in the wilderness] that might be touched, and that burned with fire, nor unto blackness, and darkness, and tempest, and the sound of a trumpet, and the voice of words; which voice they that heard entreated that the word should not be spoken to them any more;" "but ye are come unto Mount Zion, and unto the city of the living God, the heavenly Jerusalem, and to an innumerable company of angels, to the general assembly and church of the first-born which are written in heaven, and to God the Judge of all, and to the spirits of just men made perfect, and to Jesus the Mediator of the new covenant, and to the blood of sprinkling, that speaketh better things than that of Abel. See that ye refuse not him that speaketh. For if they escaped not who refused him that spake on earth, much more shall not we escape, if we turn away from him that speaketh from heaven; whose voice then shook the earth; but now he hath promised, saying, Yet once more I shake not the earth only, but also heaven. And this word, Yet once more, signifieth the removing of those things that are shaken, as of things that are made, that those things which cannot be shaken may remain."

The passage signifies that when the shaking comes, all things transient, all things secular, will pass away, while the eternal verities, the great spiritual facts, will remain, and will never change.

"Wherefore we, receiving a kingdom which cannot be moved [the great kingdom of the soul, in which reside the moral sentiments and the affections], let us [having a knowledge of this kingdom, and believing that we are moving toward the highest development of it] have grace, whereby we may serve God acceptably, with reverence and godly fear."

PRAYER.

Our Father, we pray for thy blessing. Put thine hand upon our head, and call us thy children. Warm our hearts with thy love. Grant, we pray thee, that this day we may walk with serenity of thought, with patience, and with that hope by which we are to be saved. May we be able to leave behind things that belong to the past; may we not be discontented with the things that are of the present; and may we look forward with a perpetual clearness of vision upon the things which lie before us in the future. Grant that we may have such an overruling sense of the divine power and majesty, of the nature of God, that we shall know no fear, and stand immutable.

Bless, we pray thee, all who go forth, and all who abide at home. Sanctify our intercourse. Grant that we may learn so to carry ourselves with ourselves that we shall be able at last to join with the great throng where there is no clashing; where no discords can come; where joys are harmonious and constant. We pray that thou wilt make us more fruitful in bringing before ourselves the city—*our* city. Grant that we may have more power to reproduce before us *our* God. May there be to each one a God dear to him, personal, real, all-powerful. Wilt thou stay our thoughts on thee, and satisfy our hearts in thee. May our faith in thee not take us away from each other, but strengthen our confidence in one another, and give us more gladness each in the others. So may our life be in God that it may be in each other, and with all our fellow-men.

We pray for those who are absent from us—our children; our children's children; our brothers and sisters; our companions in labor and toil; our partners in any relations of life. We pray that grace may abound toward every one.

Accept our morning offering; and carry us through every day of our lives, until at last the gates shall be thrown open, and amid shouts we shall enter, to be forever with the Lord.

We ask it in the name of the Beloved. *Amen.*

VI.
PICTURES OF TRUTH.

HYMN.

(PLYMOUTH COLLECTION, NO. 346.)

Rock of Ages, cleft for me,
Let me hide myself in Thee!
Let the water and the blood,
From Thy riven side which flowed,
Be of sin the double cure;
Cleanse me from its guilt and power.

Not the labors of my hands
Can fulfill thy law's demands:
Could my zeal no respite know,
Could my tears for ever flow,
All for sin could not atone;
Thou must save, and Thou alone!

Nothing in my hand I bring,
Simply to Thy cross I cling;
Naked, come to Thee for dress;
Helpless, look to Thee for grace;
Foul, I to Thy fountain fly;
Wash me, Saviour, or I die!

While I draw this fleeting breath,
When my eyelids close in death,
When I soar to worlds unknown,
See Thee on thy judgment throne,
Rock of Ages, cleft for me,
Let me hide myself in Thee.

VI.

PICTURES OF TRUTH.

SATURDAY MORNING, *Sept.* 12, 1874.
LESSON: Rev. v.

"I saw in the right hand of him that sat on the throne a book written within and on the back side, sealed with seven seals."

It was a roll,—a book, not in our sense of the term, but in the ancient,—and could be written, like a sheet of paper, on both sides.

" And I saw a strong angel proclaiming with a loud voice, Who is worthy to open the book, and to loose the seals thereof?"

It is not possible for us, with our western habits, to fall into the state of mind which first produced the oriental mode of symbolism, and then was educated by it—using a tower to signify a city; using an urn to signify a river; using various beasts of the field to signify certain moral qualities or important personages. We do it as a matter of ornamentation, or for a rhetorical purpose ; but with them it was a fundamental principle, a part of the scheme of their education. It was radical with them. It was to them what the letters of the alphabet, which are symbols of sounds and words, are to us. It seems very strange to talk about a lion signifying personage, but when they figuratively used the term "lion" what they thought of was a man, with all a lion's royal qualities of power, courage, superiority. When we use it we think of the thing itself in its literal sense, and then by special effort of the imagination we transfer the qualities ; whereas when they used it they thought only of the thing which was represented by it. "Crowns," "kings," "locusts," "lambs," "vials," "harps," "odors," "smoke"

—these things when spoken of in Revelation are truths to the imagination, and are meant to suggest, as they did to the ancients, not the material objects of which they are the names, but spiritual things.

"One of the elders saith unto me, Weep not; behold the Lion of the tribe of Judah, the Root of David, hath prevailed to open the book, and to loose the seven seals thereof. And I beheld, and lo, in the midst of the throne and of the four beasts, and in the midst of the elders, stood a Lamb as it had been slain (that everlasting symbol in the Jewish service, the slaying of the lamb), having seven horns, and seven eyes, which are the seven Spirits of God sent forth into all the earth."

In olden times the number seven had connected with it some mystic idea. If you come to draw, as some old painters did, a lamb with seven horns, and with seven eyes stuck all over its head, it is ludicrous; but such were the designations which came down through the Jewish history to represent the ideal man; and if you regard them as representing divine elements; if you read with your mind glancing from the symbol to the seven horns and seven eyes as representing power, and insight, and knowledge, and other elements which constitute the seven Spirits of God sent forth into the earth; if you take them in that generalizing way, you fall more nearly into the line of the understanding of those for whom the Revelation was written. The *Lamb* signified that unknown center toward which all conceivable symbolizations had been pointed.

"And he came and took the book out of the right hand of him that sat upon the throne."

Of course that is to be taken not literally, but representatively.

"And they sung a new song, saying, Thou art worthy to take the book, and to open the seals thereof; for thou wast slain, and hast redeemed us to God by thy blood out of every kindred, and tongue, and people, and nation; and hast made us unto our God kings and priests; and we shall reign on the earth. And I beheld, and I heard the voice of many angels round about the throne, and the beasts, and the elders; and the number of them was ten thousand times ten thousand, and thousands of thousands, saying with a loud voice, Worthy is the Lamb that was slain, to receive power, and riches, and wisdom, and strength, and honor, and glory, and blessing."

The disclosure of the divine beauty and wisdom and excellence in the other life is such as strikes a thrill through the universe of God.

"And every creature which is in heaven, and on the earth, and under the earth, and such as are in the sea, and all that are in them, heard I saying, Blessing, and honor, and glory, and power, be unto him that sitteth upon the throne, and unto the Lamb forever and ever."

I suppose there was never a dramatic representation that gave such a sense of the ecstacy produced by the presence of God and the universality of it as this, or that equaled it.

REMARK: Those "four beasts" spoken of—[MR. BEECHER: I never call them *beasts*—I always call them *creatures*], I have heard called living symbols—symbols of intense vitality—in animals, and birds, and all kinds of life.

MR. BEECHER : These figures are used very much as paint is. If you take a large oil painting by a master—representing magnificent warriors and heroes, for instance—you single out some steed, perhaps, that appears to have fire in his eye ; and you say, "What a wonderful expression there is in that eye !" And you go and look at it ; but when you come near it, you see that there is nothing but a daub, a little dash of the brush, where the fire seemed to be ; and the more you magnify it with a microscope, the more absurd it becomes. In itself it is nothing but a little whisk of the brush ; but when it is seen at a distance, and the imagination is brought to bear upon it, it looks like the eye of a mighty steed raised up with great enthusiasm.

REMARK: There was a colored girl in Hartford who, when talking about the Bible, said she did not like some parts of it because she could not understand them, but that she liked the Revelations because she could understand them. There is no book in the Bible that was understood to such purpose by the slaves of the South through all their troubles as the book of Revelation, because they perceived that these living images meant something good to them. They did not ask to understand them as we try to; they were merely lifted up and comforted by them. To them, in their simplicity and childlikeness, they were as a poem or as music. You meet the splendid imagery of the Revelations among the colored people of the South constant y. I recollect old Cudjo who had fenced in a piece of ground in our neighborhood [in Florida], and worked upon it, supposing it was his. He had split "tree tousand rail heself;" and a man came in, and, by some fraud of title, took the land, his "tree tousand rail," and everything, and ordered him off. He had one bale of cotton that he had raised, and that was all he got for the land. In telling of it, he said,

"Dat man come and say, 'You go off dis land.' Den I say, 'Dis my land: I bought it.' He say, 'Go off from it.' Den I say, 'Dese tree tousand rail I split ebery one mysel.' 'Can't help it,' he say; 'you go off.' 'I get it back agin,' I say. 'No, you won't,' he say. 'Yes, I will, by-and-by,' I say. He say, 'I don't know you.' I say, 'You don't know me, but de Lord, he know me; and one ob dese days de angel Gabrel come, wi' one foot on de sea, and one on de land, and he blow once for ole Uncle Cudjo.'" He understood Revelations, and the thought that the angel would blow once for him quite comforted him. About two weeks afterward, by the intervention of some of the neighbors, who knew that Cudjo was an honest man, it was ascertained that his oppressor had not made out the fulfilment of the law, and they made it out at Washington in behalf of Cudjo, and his land was restored to him; so he said that the angel blew quicker than he expected!

MR. BEECHER: You will find precisely that, where men of high moral enthusiasm are brought up under a despotism. You will find in every age, and all over the world, as in the case of the Waldenses and Huguenots, and Puritans and Scotch Covenanters, that when men are cut off from society-institutions and earthly helps they are apt to go back to the prophets in the Old Testament, or to Revelation in the New, or to both of them. Persons who are cut off from all ordinary and reasonable expectation betake themselves to the shadowy land of mysticism, and carry themselves through the most tremendous crises of human experience on the appeal of God to their imagination, or to their moral sense through their imagination, and not on the appeal of God to their conscience through their reason.

Now, New England has one fundamental heresy. The typical New England man thinks that everything in God's universe can be reduced to an idea, and expressed in an intellectual form. New Englanders, therefore, are always attempting to take the marrow out of things. As we take the crab, and suck the marrow out of each particular joint, so they take every figure, illustration and symbol in the prophecies or in Revelation, and want to crush it, and squeeze out the marrow that is in it, and bring it into the form of an intellectual statement; but that is absolutely impossible. It is absurd.

REMARK: When we were going down the Ochlochony river, the boatmen sung the book of Revelation pretty much through, one night, to the chorus, "I John saw." One man rehearsed the text, and they all came in like thunder with, "I John saw." They told about getting the dragon down from heaven, and shutting him in hell, and locking the door, and carrying the key to Jesus, and so on. There is another song taken from Revelation, where a warrior is described as being sent forth from heaven and riding on a white horse. It is one of the most solemn songs that I have ever heard. There is something in it about a dress parade, and about calling for "valiant sol-di-ers."

QUESTION: I have in my mind one notable exception to what you said about Revelation being an inspiration to good men. How can you explain Luther's idea of Revelation? Why was it that he never seemed to appreciate it, although he was under such stringent pressure?

MR. BEECHER: Well, he did not—that is all. It always seemed to me a remarkable fact.

QUESTION: It seems to me that the New England error is not, as you say, in the general belief that everything can be reduced to an intellectual idea, but in the false supposition that it is in the power of any man or any combination of men to reduce everything *in the present life* to an intellectual idea.

MR. BEECHER: Well, can you reduce music to an intellectual idea?

REMARK: I think the Lord can.

MR. BEECHER: I do not see how you can think the Lord can unless you take the boyish view that the Lord can do everything. When we children used to discuss the subject, Charles insisted that the Lord could not do everything—for instance that he could not make a sheet of paper with only one side to it!

QUESTION: That is an illustration from an entirely different class of things. We are taught that in the other life we shall have no physical body, that there will be only a soul; but do you not suppose, though there may be no sound of music, that the idea of music will remain?

MR. BEECHER: The proposition lies in its being reduced to an intellectual form of statement. It does not follow that our intellect will be the same in the other life that it is here. We know that much that we learn is higher than that which we learn by the perception of material and physical qualities, and through the reasoning intellect. We know perfectly well that what we call the intuition, or the imagination, takes in things which it is impossible for the intellect to comprehend. The intellect, as we have it here, is adapted simply to the conditions of this lower state; but when we rise into the other life we shall have a different intellect. There, instead of reducing music, or higher truths of any kind, to the form of statement by our earthly intellect, we shall have an intellect which will reject such mechanical or formal propositions, and intuitively apprehend all manner of glorious qualities and truths. Then we shall think by feeling, and not feel by thinking.

I am distinctly conscious, in preaching, when my health is perfectly good, and my subject is congenial to me and adapted to my nature, of rising into states in which I have an outlook and insight into a realm before which words are as powerless as hands are to grasp the landscape on the other side of the mountain. The truth, under such circumstances, is more clear to my inward vision than is anything that I see or hear or feel to my outward senses. I apprehend things that are absolutely non-expressible by any human words. I experience what may be likened to the opening of a window into heaven; and it gives me a feeble conception of what the future may be.

QUESTION: Is not that implied in the Thirteenth of Corinthians?

MR. BEECHER: Yes. Paul there tells us that the sum of all our knowledge in this life is so fragmentary that in comparison with the knowledge of the other life it is what the imperfect notions of childhood are in comparison with the ideas of manhood. When we die, and go into the other life, we shall look back upon the sum total of our knowledge on earth as in old age we look back upon our childish plays. There is something of truth in everything that we remember about childhood; but as measured by the more perfect knowledge of manhood it is fragmentary.

QUESTION: Does he not say that it is in the direction of feeling rather than of intellect?

MR. BEECHER: His words are:

"We know in part, and we prophesy in part; but when that which is perfect is come, that which is in part shall be done away."

There will be something left, after that which is shifting and evanescent, after the froth, is off; and it will be something substantial. What is it? Faith, hope, love, the greatest of them being love. That is going to stand the wreck of time, and dissolution, and change, and evolution, and will be found potential.

REMARK: It cannot die out; but it may take new forms of apprehension.

MR. BEECHER: Yes.

REMARK: I did not mean to say that in the future life we would reason out processes by which music would have the same peculiarities it does here, but that we should have a clearer conception of it.

MR. BEECHER: It seems to me more like instantaneity of comprehensive thought. At midnight undertake to examine a landscape with a candle, carrying it round to each particular thing, and try thus to get an idea of the whole scene. That is the way we are exploring in this life. But let a thunder-storm comes up, and a flash of lightning opens the whole country—hill, valley, cliff, every part—to instantaneous view; and we see it instantly. That is the way we will think in the other life.

PRAYER.

WE thank thee that thou hast caused the sun to shine on the earth, and reveal the beauties thereof, and that all things come forth strong and hopeful. We rejoice that it lights all things alike—the most humble and the most exalted; the poorest and the richest; the most miserable and the happiest. Unconscious of its bounty, it follows them and nourishes them; and many there be that in all their lives give no thought back to the source of their health, strength, and joy. So art thou shining in the greatness of thy love, and power, and wisdom, moulding the things of time, and looking upon the earth as a cradle where thou art rocking thy little infant ones, beholding men in their career of weakness, and want, and temptation, and in their feeble attempt at repentance and recovery. Thou art a God more merciful than the most merciful, more tender than the most tender, and more loving than the most loving, among men. Thou that hast before thee all truth and purity, dost abhor untruth and impurity. The discord of wickedness thou dost abhor; and yet thou art one that is able to prescribe a remedy for all that is evil. Thou art a God of infinite patience and long-suffering, and art bringing back to power, and beauty, and strength, and goodness, those that are afar off, and that are weak, and faint, and unlovely, and imperfect.

Deliver us in thine own way out of the peculiar troubles, and temptations, and trials that belong severally to us; or, if it be not in thy sight best that we should be delivered, then grant that we may have that which is better than deliverance—the power to endure, and to live on the bright and joyous side of our life, though there be sorrow beneath.

We pray that thus, while there may be underneath the everlasting sadness and sorrow of souls yet enchained and suffering by reason of evil, there may break out above, joyously, hymns of praise and far-reaching hopes, and more blessed visions of the imagination, and yearnings and longings that draw us upward; and as the sun shining upon the trees is felt by the roots that are buried deep in the earth, and that never see the light which brings forth from them that which is the nourishment of the whole tree, and that produces the bud, and the leaf, and the blossom that cover it; so grant that the shining of thy face upon us may reach down to the deepest parts of our nature, and that every element of our life may be so penetrated with thine influence that we may bear fruit to thine honor and glory.

Grant, we pray thee, that this day we may walk as the children of God. Why should we go shuffling and crouching through life, who are the children of the King? We belong to the aristocracy of the universe. All things are ours because we are Christ's. The victory is already won for us. We are waiting; we are traveling; we are going home to the glory that is reserved for us. May we not, therefore, be so blinded and bowed down earthward as not to see what our wealth is, or what our honors, and dignities, and joys are. Grant that we may, living in these inspiring thoughts, sustain ourselves as they that are swinging on the sea, sick in heart and body, sustain themselves by thoughts of the home which they are approaching. Looking forward to the land beyond, where thou dwellest, may we patiently wait for it, until thou callest us thither to live in thy presence.

And to thy name shall be the praise, Father, Son, and Spirit, evermore. *Amen.*

VII.
SCRIPTURE LESSON;
Without Comment.

HYMN.

(PLYMOUTH COLLECTION, NO. 704.)

Let saints below in concert sing
 With those to glory gone:
For all the servants of our King
 In earth and heaven are one.

One family, we dwell in Him,
 One church above, beneath,
Though now divided by the stream,
 The narrow stream of death:

One Army of the living God,
 To his command we bow;
Part of the host have crossed the flood,
 And part are crossing now.

Some to their everlasting home
 This solemn moment fly;
And we are to the margin come,
 And soon expect to die.

Oh, that we now might see our Guide!
 Oh, that the word were given!
Come, blessed Lord! the waves divide
 And land us all in heaven.

VII.

MONDAY MORNING, *Sept.* 14, 1874.
LESSON: Phil. ii. 1–16. Without comment.

PRAYER.

WE rejoice, our Father, that we have no need to supplicate thee to draw thine attention, to warm thine heart, or to remind thee of aught. Thou art beforehand by all the power of thy life; and we live because we are found of thee; and we love because we are melted by thy heart. We draw near to thee because thou hast drawn near to us.

We pray that thou wilt grant unto us a realization of all that thou art, or of all that thou art which is comprehensible by us. Grant that we may live in that part of ourselves where we shall understand the things of heaven. Grant that we may have that element that is of thyself in us quickened and made strong, so that it may interpret to us something of the height and depth and length and breadth of that love which passeth all understanding.

We beseech of thee, therefore, that thou wilt mould our natures; that thou wilt teach us day by day; and that we may learn to feel that by all the things that bear upon the body, and upon the heart, and upon the understanding, thou, the great Worker, art fashioning us and drawing us away from our inferior selves, and from that which is of the earth and purely earthly, and beginning in us that diviner life which shall yet grow stronger and stronger in the land that is now open to us—a land of vision, but a land which shall become our eternal home, and a land in which, when we reach it, we shall be safe.

Have compassion, we pray thee, upon every one in thy presence, and speak to each one by name, so that he may know that Christ thinks of him, that Christ loves him, and that the Spirit is manifesting itself and influencing him. May we understand thy purpose, and thy mode of dealing with us, so that we may not seem to be struggling with a host of adversaries in vain, but may behold ourselves surrounded by a cloud of witnesses and helpers. May our eyes be touched, and enabled to see the whole heaven filled with the chariots of God. May we know every day, even in sorrow, when bowed down, when the storm sweeps over us, and we are not able to stand up, that God is in the storm, and that, by-and-by, he will restore the light of his countenance to us. May we accept care and trouble and disappointment as necessary. Though for a time chastisement is not joyous but grievous, may we feel assured that afterward it will work in us the peaceable fruits of righteousness. May we be willing to be chastised, and may the assurance, that whom thou lovest thou chastenest, reconcile us to our lot. May our will from day to day be thy will. May our life seem to us as ordained of God. May it be our joy that he that hath kept us hitherto will keep us to the end, and that we shall finally be saved.

Bless, we pray thee, all this household. We thank thee for the pleasant hours that we have had together, and for the friendships which have begun between us; and we pray that those who are going forth from us from day to day, and this day, may go with a consciousness of thy providence above them and around them. May they go forth as the children of God; and may they be abundantly blessed in returning to their dear friends, to find them safe, and to be made conscious of the goodness of God in the protection of those that have been absent from them.

We pray that, as we are pilgrims on earth, and are seeking now a better place and home, we may feel that our life here is but a pilgrimage, and that our home is beyond the sea upon that shore upon which dash no waves, on which fall no storms, in whose sky is no cloud, and where is perfect blessedness evermore. There may we never be dissevered. There may we meet to rejoice in each other with an overflowing joy, and above all to rejoice in him who loved and gave himself for us, and has redeemed us unto himself.

And to the Father, the Son, and the Spirit shall be praises evermore. *Amen.*

VIII.
CHRISTIAN LIVING.

HYMN.

("SHINING SHORE.")

My days are gliding swiftly by,
  And I, a pilgrim stranger,
Would not detain them as they fly,
  Those hours of toil and danger!
    For oh, we stand on Jordan's strand,
    Our friends are passing over,
    And, just before, the shining shore
    We may almost discover.

We'll gird our loins, my brethren dear,
  Our distant home discerning;
Our absent Lord has left us word,
  Let every lamp be burning—
    For oh, we, etc.

Should coming days be cold and dark,
  We need not cease our singing;
That perfect rest none can molest
  Where golden harps are ringing.
    For oh, we, etc.

Let sorrow's rudest tempest blow,
  Each cord on earth to sever,
Our King says, Come, and there's our home,
  Forever, oh, forever!
    For oh, we, etc.

VIII.
CHRISTIAN LIVING.

LESSON: Rom. xii.

TUESDAY MORNING, Sept. 15, 1874.

"I beseech you therefore, brethren, by the mercies of God, that ye present your bodies a living sacrifice, holy, acceptable unto God, which is your reasonable service."

A sacrifice, in the Jews' estimation was the highest act of devotion. *Sacrifice* was a familiar term with them, being a part of their accustomed and daily life.

"And be not conformed to this world; but be ye transformed by the renewing of your mind, that ye may prove what is that good, and acceptable, and perfect will of God."

In Philippians he says :

"Finally, brethren, whatsoever things are true, whatsoever things are honest, whatsoever things are just, whatsoever things are pure, whatsoever things are lovely, whatsoever things are of good report; if there be any virtue, and if there be any praise, think on these things."

When we are not conformed to this world, but are transformed by the renewing of our minds, we are not to be conformed to selfishness, and pride, and frivolity, and all manner of wallowing passions; we are to be conformed only to the things which the world has found out to be good. It is not only right to be conformed to these, but the explicit command is :

"Be ye transformed by the renewing of your mind, that ye may prove what is that good, and acceptable, and perfect will of God. For I say, through the grace given unto me, to every man that is among you, not to think of himself more highly than he ought to think; but to think soberly, according as God hath dealt to every man the measure of faith."

The standard on which we are to measure ourselves, then,

is not our physical strength, or beauty; it is not our aptitude for business; the true measure of manhood is the possession of higher moral qualities. According as God hath dealt to every man the *measure of faith*, let him think of himself;—and by that rule we mostly should think very little of ourselves!

"For as we have many members in one body in Christ, and all members have not the same office: so we, being many, are one body in Christ, and every one members one of another. Having then gifts differing according to the grace that is given to us, whether prophecy, let us prophesy according to the proportion of faith."

Here prophecy does not mean foretelling, but instructing. The prophets were teachers, mainly, and they revealed the future only incidentally and occasionally. Their main office was instruction; and *prophecy* in the New Testament very largely means teaching of the higher grade—the teaching which comes from inspiration.

"Or ministry, let us wait on our ministering; or he that teacheth [catechetically], on teaching; or he that exhorteth, on exhortation."

That is, let every man be contented to develop his life along the line of those qualities and faculties in which he excels.

Do not be coveting each other's gifts. Do not refuse to do a humble thing because you cannot do a higher thing. Take that capacity which is in you, high, middle or low, and use it; and as the Apostle proceeds to show, it is more than necessary that you should do right with it. The quality of being right is important, and the quality of the right thing done is important.

"He that giveth, let him give with simplicity."

It is not enough to give. Giving must be done unaffectedly, naturally, easily, pleasantly; not in a puffed-up, arrogant and patronizing manner; not with a pompous complacency. Let him that gives do it just as quietly and naturally as he would talk. Anybody that has ever had to collect money for charitable purposes knows the difference between kind giving and giving with selfishness. Some people give; but they are always like a pump that is run down, and you have to work for an hour before you can catch the water; and then you get but little out of them. Some give; but they give only after a long argument to show how poor they are. Others give, and do it in a very showy way, so as to make the recipient feel as if he had received a great favor. But now and then you find a person who in giving to you makes you really happy. He gives promptly and sweetly; and you almost feel as though you had done *him* a favor. That is *Christian* giving.

"He that worketh, with diligence."

A slack administration is contrary to Christian morality.

"He that showeth mercy, with cheerfulness."

Some persons run at you like a dog with his mouth open; and they think that they have shown you mercy because at last they turn away and do not bite you. But mercy is to be beautiful and gracious. It is to be bestowed not surlily but with cheerfulness.

"Let love be without dissimulation."

Do not pretend to love people, for the sake of getting something from them, or for the sake of allaying their suspicion or jealousy, or anything of that kind: let love be honest.

"Abhor that which is evil; cleave to that which is good."

These chapters in the New Testament contain an ideal of life. They are so full of practical wisdom that I marvel that in all the new-fangled notions and theories and systems which set aside religion as of no account, men do not see the errors.

Contrast this twelfth chapter of Romans with any part of Solomon's Proverbs, and see the advance that has been made in the art of noble and manly living. Solomon's Proverbs are very wise indeed for the economic and practical conduct of men in exterior life; and they are very important: but they are not very deep. In this twelfth chapter of Romans the standpoint is the very interior life of a renewed manhood; and no man can follow such a chapter as this and not become simply heroic. It is a chapter of heroism.

"Be kindly affectioned one to another, with brotherly love; in honor preferring one another."

Well we do honor one another in a very small way of politeness. A well-bred person rises and gives up his seat to a superior. He would like it himself; but still the impulse of polite consideration requires that he should yield it. The young, if they are polite, will give up their seat to older persons. A gentleman will give up his seat to a lady. In a few minor things we obey this command as a particular act of politeness; but we refuse or neglect to do it in higher relations and more important elements of life.

"Not slothful in business."

Industry is a Christian virtue.

'Fervent in spirit."

Fervency is entirely reconcilable with the most industrious and enterprising business life; but it is more than enterprise and industry. Much is required of a man of which he is not capable when his feelings are cold. You cannot weld together two pieces of iron unless they are hot; but when they are at a white heat you may weld them firmly. Many elements that will not dissolve in cold water will in hot water. There are many things that you can do at a heat that you cannot do in coldness. There are many things that you cannot understand in a sluggish cold state which you can understand in a state of warmth and excitement. There are many things that a man cannot believe or do except when his soul is roused up and his imagination is flashing, and he is fervent in every part of his being. In the most fervent life things become easy, and they also become comprehensible.

"Serving the Lord."

Serve the Lord in all that you do.

"Rejoicing [when you have nothing else to rejoice in] in hope."

Live in the future when the present is intolerable. The future is that which lies along the path-walk of Christ, where the promises are.

"Patient in tribulation."

It shuts off all complaints, and repining and moroseness and combativeness.

"Continuing instant in prayer."

This means, not going down on your knees all the time, not praying by the yard or by the clock, but being in the spirit of communion with God, and pouring your thoughts, as if you had a companion close by you, into his bosom continually.

"Distributing to the necessities of the saints; given to hospitality. Bless them which persecute you: bless, and curse not. Rejoice with them that do rejoice, and weep with them that weep."

It is not demanded that we shall not sing, or that we shall not go and sit down and be merry with young folks. Paul was not of that mind. It is right, beautiful and manly to yield yourself to all right impulses in the society of those that are with you, amusing and being amused. It is proper to enjoy leisure with those that have leisure, to work with those that work, and to do business with those that do business; but we are also to sympathize with the sorrows of those who are in trouble, and to weep with them that weep.

"Be of the same mind one toward another. Mind not high things."

Do not ask, "What is the style? What is the fashion? and, What does society think?" Have a just and equitable mind which shall perceive the nature and true value of things everywhere.

"Condescend to men of low estate."

Do not, however, let them know that you are condescending, or you will spoil it all.

"Be not wise in your own conceits.

It is said, in another place, "Seest thou a man wise in his own conceit? there is more hope of a fool than of him." In still another place it is said,

"Though thou shouldest bray a fool in a mortar among wheat with a pestle, yet will not his foolishness depart from him."

And I think you might bray and pound and pestle a man that is self-conceited, and he would come out about as conceited as ever. Conceit is apt to grow stronger and stronger as men grow older. Men's tempers are softened and made sweeter by sorrows; but a man who is constitutionally and educationally self-conceited gets worse and worse as he advances in years, and becomes in old age careless in his self-conceit.

"Recompense no man evil for evil. Provide things honest in the sight of all men."

It is necessary not only to be honest, but to be known to be honest.

"If it be possible, as much as lieth in you, live peaceably with all men."

"Seek peace and pursue it," as it is said elsewhere. It is not possible to be peaceable always. "Whatsoever thy hand findeth to do, do it with thy might," I suppose would be applicable here.

"*If it be possible*, as much as lieth in you, live peaceably with all men. Dearly beloved, avenge not yourselves, but rather give place unto wrath; for it is written, Vengeance is mine [God never lent it out]; I will repay, saith the Lord. Therefore if thine enemy hunger [do not stop and commence a quibbling argument about justice] feed him; if he thirst, give him drink [and do not do it in order to heap coals of fire on his head]; for in so doing thou shalt heap coals of fire on his head."

Nothing will make him so ashamed of himself as to see how much better you behave than he did.

"Be not overcome of evil, but overcome evil with good."

PRAYER.

O God, we are ashamed when we think how long we have known thy law, and how it has been brought home to us in every specification, and with all familiarity, to see how little we have done. We have sought for knowledge that is afar off; we have been anxious to know the circuits of thy thought; we have reasoned upon infinite themes; and we have puffed ourselves up with thinking that we had knowledge; but that which pertains to the life of Christ in our souls, self-government, the development of love in all its forms, and the reduction in daily life of all our powers to thy will—how little have we learned of these things! We are not responsible before thee for that which we receive at thy hand, but only for the use which we make of it; yet how poorly have we used thine instruments that have been placed in us.

We thank thee for the blessedness of the past, and pray for the inspiration of the future. We pray that we may have discernment to know what are the things that are most important, and that we may treat thy word as the word of God, and not stop upon the letter, nor upon its external history. May we take from thy word its marrow—that which shall go to the interior and very spirit of our life.

Grant unto us this day that we may walk in the fear of the Lord, not servilely, but filially, in love, in trust, in faith, in hope. Grant that we may have joy in thee; and may it be a joy that shall reflect its light again upon all things outward, so that from the light of God in-dwelling we may have light upon our path. Grant that we may not carry our own burden. Since we have everlasting strength, may we lean upon it. May we not seek to defy the storm and the tempest: may we rather run in to the tower, to the refuge, and be hidden from the storm till it be overpast.

We pray that we may not be in despondency or despair. May we rejoice in hope. May our patience never fail. May we never feel that we have borne long enough. If thou dost forgive until seventy times seven, grant that we may bear and endure every check or hindrance or infelicity or punishment or suffering so long as it is the will of God; and may we so far conquer the inaptitude of our nature as at last to be able to rejoice in tribulations, in infirmities, in whatever shall make us manly and ennoble us with those qualities which are like thine.

We pray that thou wilt bless our households, our children, our brothers and sisters, all our dear friends and companions. May the blessing of Almighty God, which makes us so rich and happy here, abound in all the places whence we have come, and whither our thoughts return hourly.

Prosper thy cause. Unite thy people. Grant that churches may not be dashed as armies one over against another. May there be a unity among all thy people, not external, but in love and patience, in faith, in hope, and in sympathy. And grant that the promises which respect the glory of God revealed upon earth may be hastened.

May the time come when light shall shine, when the sun shall no more go down, and when the everlasting daylight of God shall abide upon the earth.

And to thy name shall be the praise, Father, Son, and Spirit. *Amen.*

IX.
ONE WITH CHRIST.

HYMN.

(PLYMOUTH COLLECTION, NO. 837.)

Jesus, lover of my soul,
  Let me to thy bosom fly
While the billows near me roll,
  While the tempest still is high:
Hide me, O my Saviour, hide,
  Till the storm of life is past.
Safe into the haven guide;
  O receive my soul at last.

Other refuge have I none—
  Hangs my helpless soul on Thee;
Leave, Oh! leave me not alone,
  Still support and comfort me;
All my trust on Thee is stayed,
  All my help from thee I bring;
Cover my defenceless head
  With the shadow of thy wing.

MR. BEECHER: Let us sing another hymn, which is not the less beautiful to our Protestant hearts because it was written by a Roman Catholic. The one that we have been singing expresses the most utter and absolute clinging and yearning dependence of the soul on Christ; and here is one that interprets that dependence—the 424th.

Thou, O my Jesus, Thou didst me
  Upon the cross embrace;
For me didst bear the nails and spear,
  And manifold disgrace;

And griefs and torments numberless,
  And sweat and agony,
Yea, death itself: and all for one
  That was thine enemy.

Then why, O blessed Jesus Christ,
  Should I not love thee well?
Not for the hope of winning heaven,
  Nor of escaping hell;

Not with the hope of gaining aught,
  Not seeking a reward;
But as Thyself hast lovèd me,
  O ever-loving Lord.

E'en so I love thee, and will love,
  And in thy praise will sing;
Solely because Thou art my God,
  And my eternal King.   —FRANCIS XAVIER.

IX.

ONE WITH CHRIST.

THURSDAY MORNING, *Sept.* 17, 1874.
LESSON: John xv. 5-13.
"I am the vine, ye are the branches. He that abideth in me, and I in him, the same bringeth forth much fruit; for without me ye can do nothing. If a man abide not in me, he is cast forth as a branch, and is withered; and men gather them, and cast them into the fire, and they are burned. If ye abide in me, and my words abide in you, ye shall ask what ye will, and it shall be done unto you."

These immortal chapters, these love-words of Christ, in his last meeting with his disciples before his passion and crucifixion, cannot be interpreted from the outside toward the inside. They perish the moment you apply to them anything like material or physical figures or illustrations. Even the vine and the branches that he himself introduces are coherent, and live together by virtue of an interior life that is common to both of them—not by the bark, not by the wood, but by the sap and the vitality which are in them. We find the nearest parallel to that truth—and a very imperfect one it is—in the relations which we sustain to one another in our innermost life, in our very best hours, where persons are brought together by elective affinities—by those influences which bring together households and relatives and lovers and friends. In hours when we are in the best health, and in the most cheerful and hopeful hours, when we have a sense of being the most perfectly at one with those who are near us, and of their being in responsive moods, so that we and they are in sympathy and unity—in those hours we approach most nearly to this sense of the intersphering of souls.

Now, the words "identity" and "unity" are so stained

and saturated with material elements that everybody stumbles at this thought of oneness. How are we one with Christ? How is Christ one with God? These are questions that are frequently asked. And yet we have (I should be sorry for one who did not have) some hours in which we are introduced into the experience of soul-unity—not similarity, necessarily, certainly not identity; yet such perfect responsiveness that two souls, or even more, act as one; and it is declared that if we abide in Christ, and his works abide in us, we may ask what we will, and it shall be done unto us.

If you take a group of friends that thus intersphere with each other by their higher nature, there is no yearning greater than, " What shall I do for these others ? How can I pour out more happiness, more thought, more feeling, more of my life, for them ? " It is not the centripetal outcry of selfishness, " Who shall show *me* any good ? " It is the pouring of the soul out in words like these : " How shall I bless those those whom I love ? How shall I make them happier ? What shall I do for them ? " One is half suffocated, sometimes, from the conscious weakness in himself— from his feeling of inability to do good and make persons happy and joyful.

In such an hour as this, then, whatsoever you shall ask will be fulfilled; and it is a blessed thing; for nothing pleases love so much as to be solicited—to be asked to do something. The grand trouble with love in this world is the want of power or opportunity for expression.

"Herein is my Father glorified, that ye bear much fruit [that you become larger in that nature which you have in common with God, and that you show the traits of your Father more and more]; so shall ye be my disciples [my scholars]."

Christ constantly represents himself as a teacher ; and those that are his are simply his scholars.

"As my father loved me, so have I loved you."

The great gulf that lies between us and Christ as a spiritual and transcendent Being is passed as quick as a flash of lightning.

" Continue ye in my love. If ye keep my commandments, ye shall abide in my love [and it might be added: If ye love ye shall abide in my commandments]; even as I have kept my Father's commandments, and abide in his love. These things have I spoken unto you, that my joy might remain in you, and that your joy might be full. This is my commandment: That ye love one another as I have loved you. Greater love hath no man than this, that a man lay down his life for his friends."

So then, again, for the hundredth time, the new commandment comes out, as the center and the potential element of life. He who knows how to rise into that love of his higher nature has at his command all discretion, all intellectual perception, all taste, all relish, all sense of truth, all justice, all discipline. Whatever is needful comes to love. It is not a mere vapid state of good nature and indifference, or of good will springing from indifference. Love is girded about with all strength, and carries in its hand both the sword and the wreath ; and it is able to slay that it may make alive, and to give pain to men that it may raise them to higher joy.

In that experience of love a man has complete possession of himself, and of every part of his nature ; and all the elements of his being affiliate harmoniously in a way that they cannot in any other condition of soul. If we aim at that and live in it, then we abide in the love of Christ.

"If ye keep my commandments ye shall abide in my love." "This is my commandment, that ye love one another as I have loved you."

You must practice love on each other in order to know how to love Christ.

PRAYER.

Thou art ascended up on high, thou that art invisible; yet not to separate thyself from us; for thou art the life of the universe; and whatever is, whatever has conscious being, and whatever rejoices, draws from thee the vitality by which it is, and by which it rejoices. We are never far from thee except in our thoughts. The distance is of our own making. It is but the difference between our feeling and thine that separates us from thee. We rejoice that thy government over all thy creatures is beneficent; and whatever there is of wrath, of scowls, of storms, and of thunder, in thy nature, is remedial. We rejoice that thou art watching over all thy creatures throughout the universe in a spirit of paternal love, and that thou art willing to bear with them, yea, to bear in their place, to carry their sins and their sorrows, and that thou art desirous that they should be healed by the stripes that are put upon them here. We rejoice that thou art a painstaking and mother-loving God, and that out of thy wisdom, and patience, and goodness we have grown to the stature which we have attained. Nor are thy commandments hard. Thou dost command, not according to thy greatness and power, but in accordance with our capacities and needs. Thou dost affiliate us one with another in all the things of life, giving us opportunity and help to deny the selfishness that is in us, and to resist and overcome pride, and to conform every passion and power to the great work of unity. We pray thee, that we may have more of the power of divine life in this way. Let us seek for thee, not by the understanding, but by the heart. May we follow after God by following the divine affections. And we pray that thus, all around about us, the day may shine brighter and brighter. May our trust in thee be more implicit; and may we know that we do not trust in the proportion that we are good, but in proportion as we need thee.

Grant, we pray thee, for thine own sake, and for the sake of that which thou hast promised in thy word, that we may be perfected; that there may be in one and another the growing of the blossom that shall at last break forth into the sweet and immortal fruit of that peace which does not depart—into that high experience of blessedness with God which is not stopped by conscious imperfection and conscious sin, but which beholds itself, as God beholds it in his infinite compassion and mercy. Grant that thus we may live in a fellowship that is above the world, and have that peace which the world cannot give us, and which the world, blessed be God, cannot take away from us. And so in strifes, and if need be in tears and in anguish, may we make good our warfare, and awake in thine image, to behold thee as thou art, and with overflowing joy unite in the song of the universe, ascribing honor, and glory, and power, and majesty unto Him that sitteth upon the throne, and unto the Lamb, for ever. *Amen.*

X.

SPIRITUAL CONCEIT.

HYMN.

(PLYMOUTH COLLECTION, No. 840.)

Give to the winds thy fears;
  Hope, and be undismay'd;
God hears thy sighs, and counts thy tears,
  God shall lift up thy head.

Through waves, through clouds and storms,
  He gently clears the way;
Wait thou his time; so shall this night
  Soon end in joyous day.

Still heavy is thy heart?
  Still sink thy spirits down?
Cast off the weight, let fear depart,
  Bid every care be gone.

Far, far above thy thought
  His counsel shall appear,
When fully he the work hath wrought
  That caused thy needless fear.

What though thou rulest not!
  Yet heaven, and earth, and hell
Proclaim, God sitteth on the throne,
  And ruleth all things well!

X.

SPIRITUAL CONCEIT.

FRIDAY MORNING, *Sept.* 18, 1874.

LESSON: Luke xv. 1-32.

"Then drew near unto him all the Publicans and sinners for to hear him. And the Pharisees and Scribes murmured, saying, This man receiveth sinners, and eateth with them."

With our manners and customs it would be considered as an impertinence for us to inquire at a hotel table, or restaurant, or any public gathering, as to the moral character of any person there. So that they observe the ordinary rules of etiquette, to eat with people means very little, except that you simply eat with them; but there was in Christ's association with these persons who were considered outcasts that which offended the conscience and the taste and the religious customs of his time, and brought him under a ban. It was not that he merely preached to wicked people, as anybody might be supposed to be at liberty to do, but there can be no question that he made himself so manifestly a companion with these people,—that he exercised such a sympathy for them, that he so recognized their manhood, and so made them feel that, wonderful as he was, a person followed and looked up to, took a personal interest in each one of them,—that he offended the Jews. It was that personality among them, and that putting himself on a level with them, that was so agreeable to them on the one side, and so offensive to the Jews on the other; and the pressure of reprehension became so great that it gave rise to a train of instruction on that subject which is very remarkable. He spoke this parable:

"What man of you, having an hundred sheep, if he lose one of them doth not leave the ninety and nine in the wilderness, and go after that which is lost, until he find it? And when he hath found it, he layeth it on his shoulders, rejoicing. And when he cometh home, he calleth together his friends and neighbors, saying unto them, Rejoice with me; for I have found my sheep which was lost. I say unto you, that likewise joy shall be in heaven over one sinner that repenteth, more than over ninety and nine just persons, which need no repentance."

The teaching here is that a revelation of the divine nature has in itself a healing power, and that the restoration or elevation of men, or their growth toward perfection, is a thousand times more rejoiced in than the fact that any one of the imperfect has attained perfection, or anything like it.

"Either what woman having ten pieces of silver, if she lose one piece, doth not light a candle, and sweep the house and seek diligently till she find it? And when she hath found it, she calleth her friends and her neighbors together, saying, Rejoice with me; for I have found the piece which I had lost. Likewise, I say unto you, there is joy in the presence of the angels of God over one sinner that repenteth."

Thus far the Saviour illustrates the attitude of the divine mind toward those that have fallen below the morals of the age in which they live. Now he gives the memorable parable which contained in it a fatal stroke at the Pharisees :

"A certain man had two sons: and the younger of them said to his father, Father, give me the portion of goods that falleth to me. And he divided unto them his living. And not many days after the younger son gathered all together, and took his journey into a far country, and there wasted his substance with riotous living. And when he had spent all, there arose a mighty famine in that land; and he began to be in want. And he went and joined himself to a citizen of that country; and he sent him into his fields to feed swine.

"And he would fain have filled his belly with the husks that the swine did eat, and no man gave unto him. And when he came to himself, he said, How many hired servants of my father's have bread enough and to spare, and I perish with hunger! I will arise and go to my father, and will say unto him, Father, I have sinned against heaven, and before thee, and am no more worthy to be called thy son : make me as one of thy hired servants. And he arose, and came to his father.

"But when he was yet a great way off, his father saw him, and had compassion, and ran, and fell on his neck, and kissed him. And the son said unto him, Father, I have sinned against heaven, and in thy sight, and am no more worthy to be called thy son. But the father said to his servants, Bring forth the best robe, and put it on him; and put a ring on his hand, and shoes on his feet; and bring hither the fatted calf, and kill it; and let us eat, and be merry: For

SPIRITUAL CONCEIT. 215

this my son was dead, and is alive again; he was lost, and is found. And they began to be merry."

Thus far, like the other two parables, this is a recognition of the divine feeling and attitude toward those who have gone wrong, but who are trying to reinstate themselves and to go right again.

Now he turns to the Pharisees :

" His elder son was in the field; and as he came and drew nigh to the house, he heard music and dancing. And he called one of the servants, and asked what these things meant. And he said unto him, Thy brother is come; and thy father hath killed the fatted calf, because he hath received him safe and sound. And he was angry, and would not go in: therefore came his father out, and entreated him. And he answering said to his father, Lo, these many years do I serve thee, neither transgressed I at any time thy commandment: and yet thou never gavest me a kid, that I might make merry with my friends. But as soon as this thy son was come, which hath devoured thy living with harlots, thou hast killed for him the fatted calf. And he said unto him, Son, thou art ever with me, and all that I have is thine, it was meet that we should make merry, and be glad: For this thy brother was dead, and is alive again; and was lost and is found."

Usually in reading the parable of the Prodigal Son, the whole force is supposed to consist simply in the fall of the young man and in the paternal love which received him back again ; but that is not the half. It is not even the point of the parable. Here are contrasted, with wonderful power, two styles of livelihood—one, that of the moralist, who had observed every external command, and who was scrupulous in his morality, but in whom the natural affections were absolutely extinguished. He kept all the days and observed all the services that were prescribed ; and he had grown perfect in his obedience to the external law ; but he was stony in his better feelings. It was moral consciousness, it was rightness of outward conduct, that made him believe that he was so good, and so high above the level of common men, that he was justified in neglecting them, and even in feeling repulsion from them. This character is drawn in direct contrast with that of the dissolute young man ; and I will defy any one to read the narrative in a calm mind, and not have sympathy with the dissipated brother as against the Pharisaic older brother. At the same time, no one ever feels that in the young man's wild and dissipated life there is any excuse or palliation ; everybody feels that he was gross and wicked; everybody is repelled from his career; and yet there was heart left in him, and penitence, and out of all his wickedness and misery there arose in him a yearning for elevation. So he went back to his father with repentance and without excuse, and our hearts go with him. On the other hand, contrast with him the hard, cold, severe, stern religionist who thought so much of God and his service that he could tread under foot his younger brother, and who on his restoration felt not one single throb of gladness. You cannot help feeling repelled from such a man with indignation; and this parable is an epitome of one of the most awful teachings of the Saviour, where he checks the dispositions that go with the passions, and with all selfishness, through the higher moral sentiments and the educated reason, and substantially says, "The dissipation of the passions is worse than you think it to be, but the perversion of the higher faculties is worse than that." To be perfectly moral, to be scrupulous in the observance of every decency of society, and to lose all sympathy for men, and all care for the weak and poor and imperfect in taking care of yourself—this is more horrible to God than if you were a drunkard and a libertine. The dissipation of the top of the head is guiltier than the dissipation of the bottom. Therefore Christ looked around upon the multitude, and said to the proudest teachers and the best men of those days, "The publicans and the harlots shall enter the kingdom of heaven before you."

That is the very style into which civilization, or what is called culture, is carrying thousands of people. It is tending to separate them from their kind, and to make them believe that nobody is worthy of their notice who is not cultivated. If common people get a living by hard work, or if by reason of neglect or a strong endowment of passion they have gone wrong, good men are supercilious and contemptuous toward them. They do not feel bound to have any care or thought for the average man. Only the select, the refined, and the cultivated will they live with in reciprocity of politeness, being thoroughly selfish; and the Saviour says that that spirit is more damnable than drunkenness. It is a very dangerous thing to pervert the best faculties of a man's nature.

PRAYER.

WE thank thee, our Father, for the light which shines above all. We thank thee for the influence which pervades the universe—for we believe thy heart is felt everywhere; and whatever there is of aspiration, and yearning for higher and better things; whatever there is of sympathy and affection and kindness outreaching everywhere that there is sentient life, is of thee. As nothing grows without the light and warmth of the sun, and all things spring forth and grow in them; so thou, Sun of Righteousness, arising with healing in thy beams, hast produced life everywhere that corresponds to thine. Thou that through cycles and ages dost draw up toward thee the great race which thou hast created, art everywhere the Center, the Life, and the Light. We pray not alone that we may feel thy power as an influence of nature; but that in nature may we feel all things as influences from God.

Bless to us, we pray thee, the teaching of thy Son, our Saviour, and his example. May we walk purely as he did. May we walk in the same sympathy and benevolent labor for men that he did. May we be as unboastful as he was. May our condescension be without pride. May our kindness be without ostentation. May we study the simplicity which belongs to true life, and seek to irradiate others by shining our sweetened affections and heart-life upon them. Help us to-day to live in our better thoughts and feelings, of trust and faith and hope and love, in cheerfulness; and whatever may be the storm, may we look above it, where thou art, in thy power, in thy glory, and where are so many whom we have loved, whom we have sent before us, and who call out to us through the void space, " Come, come," everlastingly, filling the air, sanctifying the memory, warming our hearts, quickening our weak and wasting confidence, and making the future needful to us, without which we faint, as they that are in the wilderness without a fountain.

So may we live above the present and visible, and in that great unseen, where are so many whose hearts beat no more on earth, and where we are needed and waited for.

And grant, at last, when through faith and patience we have come to the end, that there may be outpouring from the celestial city a great multitude who have waited for us, to receive us, in the midst of song and exultation, into the kingdom of our Father.

And to his name shall be the praise, forever and ever. *Amen.*

XI.
CHRIST, THE PHYSICIAN.

HYMN.

(PLYMOUTH COLLECTION, No. 898.)

Nearer, my God, to Thee,
    Nearer to Thee!
E'en though it be a cross
    That raiseth me;
Still all my song shall be,—
Nearer, my God, to Thee,
    Nearer to Thee!

Though, like the wanderer,
    The sun gone down,
Darkness be over me,
    My rest a stone;
Yet in my dreams I'd be
Nearer, my God, to Thee,—
    Nearer to Thee!

Then let the way appear,
    Steps unto heaven;
All that Thou sendest me,
    In mercy given;
Angels to beckon me
Nearer, my God, to Thee,—
    Nearer to Thee!

Then with my waking thoughts
    Bright with Thy praise,
Out of my stony griefs
    Bethel I'll raise;
So by my woes to be
Nearer, my God, to Thee,—
    Nearer to Thee!

Or, if on joyful wing,
    Cleaving the sky,
Sun, moon, and stars forgot,
    Upward I fly,
Still all my song shall be,—
Nearer, my God, to Thee,
    Nearer to thee!

XI.

CHRIST, THE PHYSICIAN.

LESSON: Luke xix.   SATURDAY MORNING, Sept. 19, 1874.

"Jesus entered and passed through Jericho. And behold, there was a man named Zaccheus, which was the chief among the publicans, and he was rich."

There were two circumstances that made him rather hateful to the Jews. The publicans were taxgatherers under the Roman government. The taxes of the province were farmed out. The tetrarch was obliged to account with the Roman government for such a sum; and then, in order to reimburse himself, he sold out his tetrarchy in divisions to sub-contractors, and they extorted the sums levied from the people.

Now, he that gathers taxes violently is hateful, and always must needs be, even if he represent the home government; but this was foreign taxation; and there was a religious as well as a personal and national indignation, and there was a perpetual and bloody hatred against the Romans; and Zaccheus was the "chief"—that is, he was a superintendent. He had, we would say, a district, with subordinate taxgatherers under him; and he was rich—which was a very bad sign! In the war, when commissaries came out of the army rich it was regarded as presumptive evidence against them; when men go into office on a small salary and come out rich it invariably gives rise to some unfavorable thoughts and comments concerning them; and here was Zaccheus, a taxgatherer, and he was rich!

"He sought to see Jesus, who he was; and he could not for the press, because he was little of stature."

He had heard a great deal about Jesus, and he had a natural curiosity to look upon him; we can see him standing on tiptoe, and trying to look between people's heads.

"He ran before, and climbed up into a sycamore-tree to see him;

for he was to pass that way. And when Jesus came to the place he looked up, and saw him, and said unto him, Zaccheus, make haste and come down; for to-day I must abide at thy house."

A more surprising address, probably, to a man that had not thought of anything but curiosity, was never made.

"He made haste, and came down, and received him joyfully. And when they [that is, the great retinue of Pharisees that hovered around] saw it, they all murmured, saying, That he was gone to be guest with a man that is a sinner."

"If he has sinned, cut him off," was the feeling; "we have not sinned; we have kept the law; and if he has sinned, why that is his lookout: justice must be done."

"Zaccheus stood and said unto the Lord [evidently having heard these murmurs, and being put upon his defense], Behold, Lord, the half of my goods I give to the poor; and if I have taken anything from any man by false accusation, I restore him four fold."

He revealed the essential equity of his life. He opened his heart in order to show that his emotions, all the tendencies of his inward life, were elevated, moral, religious.

"And Jesus said unto him, This day is salvation come to this house, forasmuch as he also is a son of Abraham. For the Son of man is come to seek and to save that which was lost."

This is repeated so often, and is construed in such a narrow and technical way, that we fail to see that it is the very genius of the kingdom of heaven; that the nature of God is *curative* and *not punitive*; that "divine justice" means that administration which restores strength to weakness, and goodness to evil, and health to all forms of disease that run towards death.

You will take notice, also, that these metaphysical and technical matters which usually are introduced with us were utterly dispensed with. Zaccheus was not told that he must repent, and have his heart changed, and then have faith in the Lord Jesus Christ, as if there were these concatenated circumstances to be looked after technically. The moment the Saviour looked upon him and saw the current of his life was upward and toward God and men in the spirit of love, and that his soul was moving in the direction of the great central element of the universe, that was enough, and he pronounced salvation on his house.

PRAYER.

"OUR Father, we thank thee that thou hast caused the light of the morning to shine again. Thou art rolling away the clouds. Behind them we behold thy fair smiling face. The storms are passing. We rejoice that above all storms is that Hand which guides them, even in the darkest hours, and causes them to nourish the earth. In the midst of the utmost tribulations thou ridest in the clouds. Clouds and darkness are around about thy throne, but justice and mercy are the habitations thereof. We rise above the defenses of men, above their assaults, above all human wisdom, into the confidence of God, who is all-wise, and ineffably kind, fulfilling mercies in overmeasure, and doing exceeding abundantly more than we ask or think. How feeble are we in our best estate! How unable are we to look through the tangled affairs of life to discern the good from the evil, and to lay our plans for the future! Though thou dost employ our wisdom and experience, how fragile are we! how unqualified to stand pressure! But how canst thou bring everything that is wrong to naught! Yet thou thyself art the same yesterday, to-day and for ever. Thou turnest men to destruction, and sayest, Return, ye children of men; but thou changest not. Thou art immutable, and thy nature is benefaction. We therefore desire, not to hide ourselves beneath our own selves, but to rise evermore into the thought of God, and join ourselves to the great multitude of thy government. Thou art the universal Father of those that seek good, and that are following after thee in thy spirit.

Forgive our pride; forgive our selfishness; forgive all sordidness, all clinging to vain and worldly things, and all malign experiences, and cleanse our hearts even by thy chastisements. As thou dost cleanse the earth and the air by thy storms, so, if it be needful, send darkness, and the voice of thunder, and the cleansing of whirlwinds, in order that there may be between our souls and thee no obstruction, no poisonous vapors, but only the clear light of love, and faith, and hope; and may these abide when all knowledge passes, when all experience is done away, when all philosophy reveals its shallowness and its earth-born nature. Then, when death hath changed us and set us free from these bodies, we shall rise into the unknown and eternal home, and find abiding faith, and hope, and love, and stand surrounded by those who are filled with these divine elements, being like them, rejoicing with them, and surrounding thee ineffably blessed, to go out no more for ever.

These mercies we ask through Jesus Christ our Redeemer. *Amen.*

XII

MAN-LOVING,
THE ROAD TO GOD-LOVING.

HYMN.

(PLYMOUTH COLLECTION, NO. 776.)

Our pathway oft is wet with tears,
  Our sky with clouds o'ercast,
And worldly cares and worldly fears
  Go with us to the last;
Not to the last! God's word hath said,
  Could we but read aright:
O pilgrim! lift in hope thy head,
  At eve it shall be light!

Though earth-born shadows now may shroud
  Our toilsome path awhile,
God's blessed word can part each cloud,
  And bid the sunshine smile.
If we but trust in living faith,
  His love and power divine,
Then, though our sun may set in death,
  His light shall round us shine.

When tempest clouds are dark on high,
  His bow of love and praise
Shines beauteous in the vaulted sky,
  Token that storms shall cease.
Then keep we on with hope unchill'd,
  By faith and not by sight,
And we shall own his word fulfill'd—
  At eve there shall be light!

XII.

MAN-LOVING, THE ROAD TO GOD-LOVING.

MONDAY MORNING, *Sept.* 21, 1874.
LESSON: John xiii. 1-17.

"Now, before the feast of the passover, when Jesus knew that his hour was come that he should depart out of this world unto the Father, having loved his own which were in the world, he loved them unto the end. And supper being ended, the devil having now put into the heart of Judas Iscariot, Simon's son, to betray him, Jesus knowing that the Father had given all things into his hands, and that he was come from God, and went to God [standing in the consciousness of his grandeur and divinity, in regard to his ulterior nature, his full self, knowing that all things had been put into his hands, that he was come from God, and that he went to 'God—in that state of mind] he riseth from supper, and laid aside his garments, and took a towel, and girded himself. After that he poureth water into a basin, and began to wash the disciples' feet, and to wipe them with the towel wherewith he was girded."

It would seem as though the first disciples that he went to, very patiently and ignorantly let him do as he had a mind to; but,

"Then cometh he to Simon Peter; and Peter saith unto him, Lord, dost thou wash my feet? Jesus answered and said unto him, What I do thou knowest not now; but thou shalt know hereafter. Peter saith unto him, Thou shalt never wash my feet. Jesus answered him, If I wash thee not, thou hast no part with me."

Then, taking it very literally, and feeling that if he was to have a part, he would like to have a pretty full one, Peter said,

"Lord, not my feet only, but my hands and my head."

He looked upon it entirely from the outside.

"Jesus saith unto him, He that is washed needeth not save to wash his feet, but is clean every whit; and ye are clean, but not all."

The Saviour was here speaking in an enigmatical way, as he was very apt to do.

"For he knew who should betray him; therefore said he, Ye are not all clean. So after he had washed their feet, and had taken his garments, and was set down again, he said unto them, "Know ye what I have done unto you? Ye call me Master and Lord; and ye say well, for so I am. If I, then, your Lord and Master, have washed your feet, ye also ought to wash one another's feet. For I have given you an example, that ye should do as I have done to you. Verily, verily, I say unto you, the servant is not greater than his lord; neither he that is sent greater than he that sent him. If ye know these things, happy are ye if ye do them."

We ought to bear in mind that this is a part of the very same general history which is celebrated in the Lord's Supper; it belongs to that institution; and I do not know any reason that makes it obligatory and a duty to celebrate the Lord's Supper which does not make it obligatory and a duty to celebrate also the washing of the disciples' feet. If I thought that we were bound by an absolute command to celebrate the Lord's Supper, and that the external form of it was obligatory, I should feel bound also to practice at the same time and always the washing of the feet, as the Christian sect that call themselves *Sandemanians* do; but both of them are mere external forms, and their celebration consists of the carrying out of the principle which the one and the other indicate. The second part of the law is, "Love thy neighbor as thyself;" and the first part is, "Thou shalt love the Lord thy God with all thy heart." That symbolical action of Christ, the breaking of the bread, signified the breaking of his body, thus revealing God to them as a great sacrifice—that is, revealing the fact that God gives his time, his thought, his feeling, his love, for men, in rearing them to honor and glory, in that we are lifted up in our affection and reverence toward God; and in the other service—that of the washing of the feet—we are taught how to humble ourselves to the lowest offices of kindness; how to make ourselves less than the least, if in so doing we can help them; and I think it is a great deal harder to practice this injunction than the other. It is very easy for men to reverence God, but it is not so easy for them to recognize their neighbor, and to love him as themselves, and to fulfill all the duties which love implies, undergoing self-sacrifice, and doing things that are abasing and are repugnant to our natural pride and to our feelings. That, however, is the disclosure of the law of God. John asks, If we hate our brother, whom we have seen, how can we love God whom we have not seen? The way to right experience toward God lies through the full disclosure of love-service toward our fellow-men. It is not a substitute for the love of God; it is the avenue through which we come to the higher life; and in proportion as we practice toward our fellow-men all gentleness and sweetness and helpfulness, and sacrifice ourselves for their sakes, in that proportion we shall know how God first sacrificed himself for us, and how he is at once a Legislator and Judge and a Father, and how all these can move together in the great sphere of divine love.

PRAYER.

Vouchsafe, our Father, thy blessing to rest upon us. Thou hast blessed us, and made this place memorable. We thank thee that we have so many of us been drawn together in the better relations which include the hope and faith of the life that is to come. We thank thee for all the hours of enjoyment which we have had together, and for the enriching of our affections one in the other. We thank thee that we have been strengthened in faith and in hope, and that joy itself has been wings to faith.

Now we are to disperse, having met for the last time, so many of us, together in this place. We pray that we may do it without sadness; that we may do it with thankfulness for that which is past, and with hope for that which is to come. May we never forget that we are called, not to darkness, but to light; that we are children of the day; and that our faces should shine as those upon whom God is shining.

We pray that we may go forth to meet the duties of life, to assume its burdens and responsibilities with more trust in thee; with no trust in our own strength, which is so poor and so failing. May our hearts be stayed upon God.

Fulfill to every one of us, we beseech of thee, the promises which thou hast made. Be a defense to those that are assaulted. Open a door to those who are pursued, that they may run in and be safe. Hide them in thy pavilion until the storm be overpast. We pray that thou wilt give grace to those who are violently tempted, that they may be able to resist temptation, and come off with victory. We pray that thou wilt raise up all who are cast down and that are desponding. Wilt thou give strength to every one that is to assume burdens and carry sorrows. We beseech of thee that to those whose life is outward divine grace may be ministered in all fidelity; and that in all rectitude they may walk before men. We pray that those whose lives are hidden, and whose sorrows are unspoken, may have the witness of the spirit of God dwelling evermore in them. May those who seem to themselves to be treading their last steps on the shadowy side of life rejoice that the day is not far distant when they shall enter upon their nobler rest and life. We pray that those whose life is apparently before them may be girded with strength, and grow more and more in truth and honor and fidelity toward men.

Bless, we pray thee, the church universal. May thy disciples of every name study the things in which they agree one with another. May divisions, and oppositions, and prejudices, and hatings pass away; and may the common love of Jesus bind them together in love, that they may work together. And now that the enemy is coming in like a flood, we pray that all thy people may feel for each other's hands, and stand banded together immovable and firm for rectitude. We pray that thus the power of the Holy Ghost may overshadow all churches, and that the glory of the Lord may fill this land, even as the waters fill the sea.

We commend ourselves to thy fatherly care. May we carry away a song. May we rejoice in the Lord, and again may we rejoice. And so, singing and rejoicing in the midst of infirmities and trials, may we follow in the footsteps of those worthies who now are crowned in heaven; and may we be received with infinite greetings and rejoicings, and have an exceeding abundant entrance administered to us in the kingdom of our Father.

We ask it in the adorable name of Jesus, to whom, with the Father and the Spirit, shall be praises everlasting. *Amen.*

www.ingramcontent.com/pod-product-compliance
Lightning Source LLC
Chambersburg PA
CBHW022008220426
43663CB00007B/1006